Creation and Evolution

CREATION AND EVOLUTION
Myth or Reality?

Norman D. Newell

CONVERGENCE

**A Series Founded, Planned, and Edited by
Ruth Nanda Anshen**

PRAEGER

PRAEGER SPECIAL STUDIES • PRAEGER SCIENTIFIC

New York • Philadelphia • Eastbourne, UK
Toronto • Hong Kong • Tokyo • Sydney

Library of Congress Cataloging in Publication Data

Newell, Norman Dennis, 1909—
    Creation and evolution.

    (Convergence)
    Bibliography: p.
    Includes index.
    1. Creation. 2. Evolution. I. Title.
II. Series: Convergence (New York, N.Y.)
BS651.N46   1985   231.7′65   84-17858
ISBN 0-03-001012-8 (alk. paper)

Published in 1985 by Praeger Publishers
CBS Educational and Professional Publishing
a Division of CBS Inc.
521 Fifth Avenue, New York, NY 10175 USA
© 1982 and 1985 by Norman D. Newell
"Convergence," "The Möbius Strip," and "Foreword"
© 1981 and 1982 by Ruth Nanda Anshen

56789 052 987654321

Printed in the United States of America
on acid-free paper

To Gilli, with love

CONVERGENCE
A Series Founded, Planned, and Edited by Ruth Nanda Anshen

Books in the Convergence Series

The Double-Edged Helix
Genetic Engineering in the Real World
Liebe F. Cavalieri

Progress or Catastrophe
The Nature of Biological Science and Its
Impact on Human Society
Bentley Glass

Emerging Cosmology
Bernard Lovell

Creation and Evolution
Myth or Reality?
Norman D. Newell

Anatomy of Reality
Merging of Intuition and Reason
Jonas Salk

Science and Moral Priority
Merging Mind, Brain, and Human Values
Roger Sperry

Contents

Convergence

by

Ruth Nanda Anshen

"There is no use trying," said Alice; "one *can't* believe impossible things."

"I dare say you haven't had much practice," said the Queen. "When I was your age, I always did it for half an hour a day. Why, sometimes I've believed as many as six impossible things before breakfast."

This commitment is an inherent part of human nature and an aspect of our creativity. Each advance of science brings increased comprehension and appreciation of the nature, meaning, and wonder of the creative forces that move the cosmos and created man. Such openness and confidence lead to faith in the reality of possibility and eventually to the following truth: "The mystery of the universe is its comprehensibility."

When Einstein uttered that challenging statement, he could have been speaking about our relationship with the universe. The old division of the Earth and the Cosmos into objective processes in space and time and mind in which they are mirrored is no longer a suitable starting point for understanding the universe, science, or ourselves. Science now begins to focus on the convergence of man and nature, on the framework which makes us, as living beings, dependent parts of nature and simultaneously makes nature the object of our thoughts and actions. Scientists can no longer confront the universe as objective observers. Science recognizes the participation of man with the universe. Speaking quantitatively, the universe is largely indifferent to what happens in man. Speaking qualitatively, nothing happens in man that does not have a bearing on the elements which constitute the universe. This gives cosmic significance to the person.

Nevertheless, all facts are not born free and equal. There exists a hierarchy of facts in relation to a hierarchy of values. To arrange the facts rightly, to differentiate the important from the trivial, to see their bearing in relation to each other and to evaluational criteria, requires a judgment which is intuitive as well as empirical. Man needs meaning in addition to information. Accuracy is not the same as truth.

Our hope is to overcome the cultural *hubris* in which we have been living. The scientific method, the technique of analyzing, explaining, and classifying, has demonstrated its inherent limitations. They arise because, by its intervention, science presumes to alter and fashion the object of its investigation. In reality, method and object can no longer be separated. The outworn Cartesian, scientific world view has ceased to be scientific in the most profound sense of the word, for a common bond links us all—man, animal, plant, and galaxy—in the unitary principle of all reality. For the self without the universe is empty.

This universe of which we human beings are particles may be defined as a living, dynamic process of unfolding. It is a breathing universe, its respiration being only one of the many rhythms of its life. It is evolution itself. Although what we observe may seem to be a community of separate, independent units, in actuality these units are made up of subunits, each with a life of its own, and the subunits constitute smaller living entities. At no level in the hierarchy of nature is independence a reality. For that which lives and constitutes matter, whether organic or inorganic, is dependent on discrete entities that, gathered together, form aggregates of new units which interact in support of one another and become an unfolding event, in constant motion, with ever-increasing complexity and intricacy of their organization.

Are there goals in evolution? Or are there only discernible patterns? Certainly there is a law of evolution by which we can explain the emergence of forms capable of activities which are indeed novel. Examples may be said to be the origin of life, the emergence of individual consciousness, and the appearance of language.

The hope of the concerned authors in Convergence is that they will show that evolution and development are interchangeable and that the entire system of the interweaving of man, nature, and the universe constitutes a living totality. Man is searching for his legitimate place in this unity, this cosmic scheme of things. The meaning of this cosmic scheme—if indeed we can impose meaning on the mystery and majesty of nature—and the extent to which we can assume responsibility in it as uniquely intelligent beings, are supreme questions for which this Series seeks an answer.

Inevitably, toward the end of a historical period, when thought and custom have petrified into rigidity and when the elaborate machinery of civilization opposes and represses our more noble qualities, life stirs again beneath the hard surface. Nevertheless, this attempt to define the purpose of Convergence is set forth with profound trepidation. We are living in a period of extreme darkness. There is moral atrophy, destructive radiation within us, as we watch the collapse of values hitherto cherished—but now betrayed. We seem to be face to face with an apocalyptic destiny. The anomie, the chaos, surrounding us produces an almost lethal disintegration of the person, as well as ecological and demographic disaster. Our situation is desperate. And there is no glossing over the deep and unresolved tragedy that fills our lives. Science now begins to question its premises and tells us not only what *is*, but what *ought* to be; *pre*scribing in addition to *de*scribing the realities of life, reconciling order and hierarchy.

My introduction to Convergence is not to be construed as a prefatory essay to each individual volume. These few pages attempt to set forth the general aim and purpose of this Series. It is my hope that this statement will provide the reader with a new orientation in his thinking, one more specifically defined by these scholars who have been invited to participate in this intellectual, spiritual, and moral endeavor so desperately needed in our time. These scholars recognize the relevance of the nondiscursive experience of life which the discursive, analytical method alone is unable to convey.

The authors invited to Convergence Series acknowledge a structural kinship between subject and object, between living and nonliving matter, the immanence of the past energizing the present and thus bestowing a promise for the future. This kinship has long been sensed and experienced by mystics. Saint Francis of Assisi described with extraordinary beauty the truth that the more we know about nature, its unity with all life, the more we realize that we are one family, summoned to acknowledge the intimacy of our familial ties with the universe. At one time we were so anthropomorphic as to exclude as inferior such other aspects of our relatives as animals, plants, galaxies, or other species—even inorganic matter. This only exposed our provincialism. Then we believed there were borders beyond which we could not, must not, trespass. These frontiers have never existed. Now we are beginning to recognize, even take pride in, our neighbors in the Cosmos.

Human thought has been formed through centuries of man's consciousness, by perceptions and meanings that relate us to nature. The smallest living entity, be it a molecule or a particle, is at the same time present in the structure of the Earth and all its inhabitants, whether human or manifesting themselves in the multiplicity of other forms of life.

Today we are beginning to open ourselves to this evolved experience of consciousness. We keenly realize that man has intervened in the evolutionary process. The future is contingent, not completely prescribed, except for the immediate necessity to evaluate in order to live a life of integrity. The specific gravity of the burden of change has moved from genetic to cultural evolution. Genetic evolution itself has taken millions of years; cultural evolution is a child of no more than twenty or thirty thousand years. What will be the future of our evolutionary course? Will it be cyclical in the classical sense? Will it be linear in the modern sense? Yet we know that the laws of nature are not linear. Certainly, life is more than mere endless repetition. We must restore the importance of each moment, each deed. This is impossible if the future is nothing but a mechanical extrapolation of the past. Dignity becomes possible only with choice. The choice is ours.

In this light, evolution shows man arisen by a creative power inherent in the universe. The immense ancestral effort that has borne man invests him with a cosmic responsibility. Michelangelo's image of Adam created at God's command becomes a more intelligent symbol of man's position in the world than does a description of man as a chance aggregate of atoms or cells. Each successive stage of emergence is more comprehensive, more meaningful, more fulfilling, and more converging, than the last. Yet a higher faculty must always operate through the levels that are below it. The higher faculty must enlist the laws controlling the lower levels in the service of higher principles, and the lower level which enables the higher one to operate through it will always limit the scope of these operations, even menacing them with possible failure. All our higher endeavors must work through our lower forms and are necessarily exposed thereby to corruption. We may thus recognize the cosmic roots of tragedy and our fallible human condition. Language itself as the power of universals, is the basic expression of man's ability to transcend his environment and to transmute tragedy into a moral and spiritual triumph.

This relationship, this convergence, of the higher with the lower applies again when an upper level, such as consciousness or freedom, endeavors to reach beyond itself. If no higher level can be accounted for by the operation of a lower level, then no effort of ours can be truly creative in the sense of establishing a higher principle not intrinsic to our initial condition. And establishing such a principle is what all great art, great thought, and great action must aim at. This is indeed how these efforts have built up the heritage in which our lives continue to grow.

Has man's intelligence broken through the limits of his own powers? Yes and no. Inventive efforts can never fully account for their success, but the story of man's evolution testifies to a creative power that goes beyond that which we can account for in ourselves. This power can make us surpass ourselves. We exercise some of it in the simple act of acquiring knowledge and holding it to be true. For, in doing so, we strive for intellectual control over things outside ourselves, in spite of our manifest incapacity to justify this hope. The greatest efforts of the human mind amount to no more than this. All such acts impose an obligation to strive for the ostensibly impossible, representing man's search for the fulfillment of those ideals which, for the moment, seem to be beyond his reach. For the good of a moral act is inherent in the act itself and has the power to ennoble the person who performs it. Without this moral ingredient there is corruption.

The origins of one person can be envisaged by tracing that person's family tree all the way back to the primeval specks of protoplasm in which his first origins lie. The history of the family tree converges with everything that has contributed to the making of a human being. This segment of evolution is on a par with the history of a fertilized egg developing into a mature person, or the history of a plant growing from a seed; it includes everything that caused that person, or that plant, or that animal, or even that star in a galaxy, to come into existence. Natural selection plays no part in the evolution of a single human being. We do not include in the mechanism of growth the possible adversities which did not befall it and hence did not prevent it. The same principle of development holds for the evolution of a single human being; nothing is gained in understanding this evolution by considering the adverse chances which might have prevented it.

In our search for a reasonable cosmic view, we turn in the first place to common understanding. Science largely relies for its subject matter on a common knowledge of things. Concepts of life and death, plant and animal, health and sickness, youth and age, mind and body, machine and technical processes, and other innumerable and equally important things are commonly known. All these concepts apply to complex entities, whose reality is called into question by a theory of knowledge which claims that the entire universe should ultimately be represented in all its aspects by the physical laws governing the inanimate substrate of nature. "Technological inevitability" has alienated man's relationship with nature, with work, with other human beings, with himself. Judgment, decision, and freedom of choice, in other words *knowledge* which contains a moral imperative, cannot be ordered in the form that some technological scientists believe. For there is no mechanical ordering, no exhaustive set of permutations or combinations that can perform the task. The power which man has achieved through technology has been transformed into spiritual and moral impotence. Without the insight into the nature of *being*, more important than *doing*, the soul of man is imperilled. And those self-transcendent ends that ultimately confer dignity, meaning, and identity on man and his life constitute the only final values worth pursuing. The pollution of consciousness is the result of mere technological efficiency. In addition, the authors in this Series recognize that the computer in itself can process information—not meaning. Thus we see on the stage of life no moral actors, only anonymous events.

Our new theory of knowledge, as the authors in this Series try to demonstrate, rejects this claim and restores our respect for the immense range of common knowledge acquired by our experience of convergence. Starting from here, we sketch out our cosmic perspective by exploring the wider implications of the fact that all knowledge is acquired and possessed by relationship, coalescence, convergence.

We identify a person's physiognomy by depending on our awareness of features that we are unable to specify, and this amounts to a convergence in the features of a person for the purpose of comprehending their joint meaning. We are also able to read in the features and behavior of a person the presence of moods, the gleam of intelligence, the response to animals or a sunset or a fugue by Bach, the signs of sanity, human responsibility, and experience. At a lower level, we comprehend by a similar mechanism the body of a person and understand the functions of the physiological mechanism. We know that even physical theories constitute in this way the processes of inanimate nature. Such are the various levels of knowledge acquired and possessed by the experience of convergence.

The authors in this Series grasp the truth that these levels form a hierarchy of comprehensive entities. Inorganic matter is comprehended by physical laws; the mechanism of physiology is built on these laws and enlists them in its service. Then, the intelligent behavior of a person relies on the healthy functions of the body and, finally, moral responsibility relies on the faculties of intelligence directing moral acts.

We realize how the operations of machines, and of mechanisms in general, rely on the laws of physics but cannot be explained, or accounted for, by these laws. In a hierarchic sequence of comprehensive levels, each higher level is related to the levels below it in the same way as the operations of a machine are related to the particulars, obeying the laws of physics. We cannot explain the operations of an upper level in terms of the particulars on which its operations rely. Each higher level of integration represents, in this sense, a higher level of existence, not completely accountable by the levels below it yet including those lower levels implicitly.

In a hierarchic sequence of comprehensive levels each higher level is known to us by relying on our awareness of the particulars on the level below it. We are conscious of each level by internalizing its particulars and mentally performing the integration that constitutes it. This is how all experience, as well as all knowledge, is based on convergence, and this is how the consecutive stages of convergence form a continuous transition from the understanding of the inorganic, the inanimate, to the comprehension of man's moral responsibility and participation in the totality, the organismic whole, of all reality. The sciences of the subject-object relationship thus pass imperceptibly into the metascience of the convergence of the subject and object interrelationship, mutually altering each other. From the minimum of convergence, exercised in a physical observation, we move without a break to the maximum of convergence, which is a total commitment.

"The last of life, for which the first was made, is yet to come." Thus, Convergence has summoned the world's most concerned thinkers to rediscover the experience of *feeling,* as well as of thought. The convergence of all forms of reality presides over the possible fulfillment of self-awareness—not the isolated, alienated self, but rather the participation in the life process with other lives and other forms of life. Convergence is a cosmic force and may possess liberating powers allowing man to become what he is, capable of freedom, justice, love. Thus man experiences the meaning of grace.

A further aim of this Series is not, nor could it be, to disparage science. The authors themselves are adequate witness to this fact. Actually, in viewing the role of science, one arrives at a much more modest judgment of its function in our whole body of knowledge. Original knowledge was probably not acquired by us in the active sense; most of it must have been given to us in the same mysterious way we received our consciousness. As to content and usefulness, scientific knowledge is an infinitesimal fraction of natural knowledge. Nevertheless, it is knowledge whose structure is endowed with beauty because its abstractions satisfy our urge for specific knowledge much more fully than does natural knowledge, and we are justly proud of scientific knowledge because we can call it our own creation. It teaches us clear thinking, and the extent to which clear thinking helps us to order our sensations is a marvel which fills the mind with ever new and increasing admiration and awe. Science now begins to include the realm of human values, lest even the memory of what it means to be human be forgotten.

Organization and energy are always with us, wherever we look, on all levels. At the level of the atom organization becomes indistinguishable from form, from order, from whatever the forces are that hold the spinning groups of ultimate particles together in their apparent solidity. And now that we are at the atomic level, we find that modern physics has recognized that these ultimate particles are primarily electrical charges, and that mass is therefore a manifestation of energy. This has often been misinterpreted by idealists as meaning that matter has somehow been magicked away as if by a conjuror's wand. But nothing could be more untrue. It is impossible to transform matter into spirit just by making it thin. Bishop Berkeley's views admit of no refutation but carry no conviction nevertheless. However, something has happened to matter. It was only separated from form because it seemed too simple. Now we realize that—and this is a revolutionary change— we cannot separate them. We are now summoned to cease speaking of Form and Matter and begin to consider the convergence of Organization and Energy. For the largest molecule we know and the smallest living particles we know overlap. Such a cooperation, even though far down at the molecular level, cannot but remind us of the voluntary cooperation of individual human beings in maintaining patterns of society at levels of organization far higher. The tasks of Energy and Organization in the making of the universe and ourselves are far from ended.

No individual destiny can be separated from the destiny of the universe. Alfred North Whitehead has stated that every event, every step or process in the universe, involves both effects from past situations and the anticipation of future potentialities. Basic for this doctrine is the assumption that the course of the universe results from a multiple and never-ending complex of steps developing out of one another. Thus, in spite of all evidence to the contrary, we conclude that there is a continuing and permanent energy of that which is not only man but all of life. For not an atom stirs in matter, organic and inorganic, that does not have its cunning duplicate in mind. And faith in the convergence of life with all its multiple manifestations creates its own verification.

We are concerned in this Series with the unitary structure of all nature. At the beginning, as we see in Hesiod's *Theogony* and in the Book of Genesis, there was a primal unity, a state of fusion in which, later, all elements become separated but then merge again. However, out of this unity there emerge, through separation, parts of opposite elements. These opposites intersect or reunite, in meteoric phenomena or in individual living things. Yet, in spite of the immense diversity of creation, a profound underlying convergence exists in all nature. And the principle of the conservation of energy simply signifies that there is a *something* that remains constant. Whatever fresh notions of the world may be given us by future experiments, we are certain beforehand that something remains unchanged which we may call *energy*. We now do not say that the law of nature springs from the invariability of God, but with that curious mixture of arrogance and humility which scientists have learned to put in place of theological terminology, we say instead that the law of conservation is the physical expression of the elements by which nature makes itself understood by us.

The universe is our home. There is no other universe than the universe of all life including the mind of man, the merging of life with life. Our consciousness is evolving, the primordial principle of the unfolding of that which is implied or contained in all matter and spirit. We ask: Will the central mystery of the cosmos, as well as man's awareness of and participation in it, be unveiled, although forever receding, asymptotically? Shall we perhaps be able to see all things, great and small, glittering with new light and reborn meaning, ancient but now again relevant in an iconic image which is related to our own time and experience?

The cosmic significance of this panorama is revealed when we consider it as the stages of an evolution that has achieved the rise of man and his consciousness. This is the new plateau on which we now stand. It may seem obvious that the succession of changes, sustained through a thousand million years, which have transformed microscopic specks of protoplasm into the human race, has brought forth, in so doing, a higher and altogether novel kind of being, capable of compassion, wonder, beauty, and truth, although each form is as precious, as sacred, as the other. The interdependence of everything with everything else in the totality of being includes a participation of nature in history and demands a participation of the universe.

The future brings us nothing, gives us nothing; it is we who in order to build it have to give it everything, our very life. But to be able to give, one has to possess; and we possess no other life, no living sap, than the treasures stored up from the past and digested, assimilated, and created afresh by us. Like all human activities, the law of growth, of evolution, of convergence draws its vigor from a tradition which does not die.

At this point, however, we must remember that the law of growth, of evolution, has both a creative and a tragic nature. This we recognize as a degenerative process, as devolution. Whether it is the growth of a human soul or the growth of a living cell or of the universe, we are confronted not only with fulfillment but with sacrifice, with increase and decrease, with enrichment and diminution. Choice and decision are necessary for growth, and each choice, each decision, excludes certain potentialities, certain potential realities. But since these unactualized realities are part of us, they possess a right and command of their own. They must avenge themselves for their exclusion from existence. They may perish and with them all the potential powers of their existence, their creativity. Or they may not perish but remain unquickened within us, repressed, lurking, ominous, swift to invade in some disguised form our life process, not as a dynamic, creative, converging power, but as a necrotic, pathological force. If the diminishing and the predatory processes comingle, atrophy and even death in every category of life ensue. But if we possess the maturity and the wisdom to accept the necessity of choice, of decision, of order and hierarchy, the inalienable right of freedom and autonomy, then, in spite of its tragedy, its exclusiveness, the law of growth endows us with greatness and a new moral dimension.

Convergence is committed to the search for the deeper meanings of science, philosophy, law, morality, history, technology, in fact all the disciplines in a transdisciplinary frame of reference.

This Series aims to expose the error in that form of science which creates an unreconcilable dichotomy between the observer and the participant, thereby destroying the uniqueness of each discipline by neutralizing it. For in the end we would know everything but *understand nothing*, not being motivated by concern for any question. This Series further aims to examine relentlessly the ultimate premises on which work in the respective fields of knowledge rest and to break through from these into the universal principles which are the very basis of all specialist information. More concretely, there are issues which wait to be examined in relation to, for example, the philosophical and moral meanings of the models of modern physics, the question of the purely physico-chemical processes versus the postulate of the irreducibility of life in biology. For there is a basic correlation of elements in nature, of which man is a part, which cannot be separated, which compose each other, which converge, and alter each other mutually.

Certain mysteries are now known to us: the mystery, in part, of the universe and the mystery of the mind have been in a sense revealed out of the heart of darkness. Mind and matter, mind and brain, have converged; space, time, and motion are reconciled; man, consciousness, and the universe are reunited since the atom in a star is the same as the atom in man. We are homeward bound because we have accepted our convergence with the Cosmos. We have reconciled observer and participant. For at last we know that time and space are modes by which we think, but not conditions in which we live and have our being. Religion and science meld; reason and feeling merge in mutual respect for each other, nourishing each other, deepening, quickening, and enriching our experiences of the life process. We have heeded the haunting voice in the Whirlwind.

The Möbius Strip

The symbol found on the cover of each volume in Convergence is the visual image of *convergence*—the subject of this Series. It is a mathematical mystery deriving its name from Augustus Möbius, a German mathematician who lived from 1790 to 1868. The topological problem still remains unsolved mathematically.

The Möbius Strip has only one continuous surface, in contrast to a cylindrical strip, which has two surfaces—the inside and the outside. An examination will reveal that the Strip, having one continuous edge, produces *one* ring, twice the circumference of the original Strip with one half of a twist in it, which eventually *converges with itself.*

Since the middle of the last century, mathematicians have increasingly refused to accept a "solution" to a mathematical problem as "obviously true," for the "solution" often then becomes the problem. For example, it is certainly obvious that every piece of paper has two sides in the sense that an insect crawling on one side could not reach the other side without passing around an edge or boring a hole through the paper. Obvious—but false!

The Möbius Strip, in fact, presents only one mono-dimensional, continuous ring having no inside, no outside, no beginning, no end. Converging with itself it symbolizes the structural kinship, the intimate relationship between subject and object, matter and energy, demonstrating the error of any attempt to bifurcate the observer and participant, the universe and man, into two or more systems of reality. All, all is unity.

I am indebted to Fay Zetlin, Artist-in-Residence at Old Dominion University in Virginia, who sensed the principle of convergence, of emergent transcendence, in the analogue of the Möbius Strip. This symbol may be said to crystallize my own continuing and expanding explorations into the unitary structure of all reality. Fay Zetlin's drawing of the Möbius Strip constitutes the visual image of this effort to emphasize the experience of coalescence.

R.N.A.

Creation and Evolution

Foreword

That the creationist movement in this last quarter of the twentieth century can again voice its irrational passions long legitimately silenced, so we thought, is indeed an astonishing and compelling fact. But since facts are not born free and equal, as I have said, we are summoned to consider this phenomenon in relation to the hierarchy of facts reflecting the hierarchy of values. We hereby confront the question of freedom itself.

Freedom is one of the indispensable foods of the human soul. Freedom means the ability to choose. We must understand, of course, a real ability. When the possibilities of choice are so wide as to injure the integrity of the mind and heart, reason and experience, then inevitable error takes place. The need for meaning, purpose, and fulfillment, even for happiness lies deep in the nature of man. This need has been subverted by the cultural and historical phenomenon of creationism, an accelerating rejection of science, of the evidence of evolution and a widespread anti-intellectualism. It exists by virtue of the failure of science to bestow values on the facts with which it deals. Such lack finds its expression in the yearnings of those who feel lost in an age committed to technological progress denying the needs of the spirit.

The creationist movement is a manifestation of the failure of love, of the loss of man's legitimate place in the cosmic scheme. However, the fundamentalist process is a symptom of a disease, of irrationality, a denial of reason and responsibility to truth. Its adherents are to receive our compassion for they have taken the path of error. They deceive themselves that they have chosen the way of freedom. And under these circumstances men, believing wrongly that they are in possession of freedom and feeling that they have no enjoyment nor evidence of it, end by thinking that freedom is not a good thing. Herein lies the danger of creationism and its legendary interpretation of biblical Creation.

The rejection by the creationists of evolutionary evidence is in itself a disregard of the true Good and is thus to disobey that very

God whom they proclaim to revere. They deny the absolute Good which is infinitely precious since God himself obeys the laws of the universe. He cannot make the radii of a circle unequal to each other. He too submits to contingency, to surprise, to the underivably new, in other words, to an expanding universe, to evolution. The dogmatic, literal interpretation of biblical Creation rejects its deepest meaning, its allegory, and enriching symbolism. For what makes the blind forces of matter obedient to evolutionary processes is not a decree from heaven but a law in which the divine presence may be said to exist and which it is a mortal sin to deny. By a direct effect of its continual presence, the creationists express judgments and opinions which, unknown to them, are based on standards that are contrary to the spirit of Christianity. And the most disastrous consequence of this is to make it impossible for the virtue of intellectual probity to be exercised.

R.N.A.

Preface

Biblical Creation versus evolution—this has been an acrimonious issue for well over a century between religious conservatives, especially Protestant fundamentalists, and those liberals who consider the Bible to be allegorical and symbolic. The immediate question is whether "creationism" should be regarded as a scientific theory and be taught in public schools together with, or in place of, a scientific history of the universe and life on earth. The more far-reaching implications of this question involve our attitudes toward the nature, origin, and history of the universe—scientific cosmology—and even freedom of thought.

Who are these creationists and what are their aims? They are fundamentalist Protestants who regard the Bible, and particularly the Book of Genesis, as infallible. Their aim is to have their views presented as an alternative "model" in contrast to evolution in all public school science classes. A 1976 Gallup poll found that 50 million Americans claim to be born-again Christians, and a substantial proportion of these believe the Bible's account of Creation to be factual.

Although this controversy goes back more than a century it was relatively dormant between the time of the Scopes trial in 1925 and 1960. Subsequently, a group in California organized a fresh campaign of fundamentalism (or creationism) which has since become nationwide and even international in its scope. There are now many "Creation" institutes, colleges, societies, and clubs across the country which demand of their members or faculties oaths accepting the Genesis account of Creation and the Flood as literal history.

This volume in Convergence confronts the controversy as it is today. I have written it not only for intelligent and cultivated students and laymen and women, but especially for schoolteachers, young people and their parents, and for all those whose scientific background is not adequate to withstand the high-pressure methods and the misleading arguments posed by the creationists. The leaders of these groups range in character from sincere local ministers who are genuinely but mistakenly alarmed by the idea that new scientific knowledge may inevitably lead to a loss of morals and ethics, to television evangelists and New Right and Moral Majority spokesmen such as Jerry Falwell who are more politically motivated.

In this preface I will touch only briefly on some of the creationist attitudes and assertions. In making much of the idea that scientists do not agree even among themselves about evolution, the creationists fail to distinguish between the *fact* of evolution and the theories of evolution. According to Webster's dictionary, a fact is "an occurrence, quality, or relation, the reality of which is manifest in experience or may be inferred with certainty." From many converging lines of evidence biologists and paleontologists long ago accepted organic evolution as a fact. Scientific theories, however, are not facts, but constitute scientific explanations of scientific information or knowledge. Such theories are ideas (for example, Darwin's theory of natural selection), and they are continually under study as they are used in the search for new facts and new explanations. The statements must therefore be modified from time to time in order to accommodate new discoveries resulting in new viewpoints.

One of the ideas in science that worries creationists is that man is related to animals as well as to all other forms of life. Since they believe that man, and man only, was created in the image of God, this idea of relatedness is abhorrent to them. Scientists are aware of the uniqueness of the human condition, but years of research have shown that the human species is built of much the same parts as other animals modified for different modes of life. It is the sum of the parts rather than the details that distinguishes man from the rest of the animal kingdom.

My own particular branch of science—paleontology—has been attacked vigorously by creationists on the grounds that the Book of Genesis contradicts the scientific views of an ancient, constantly changing universe and a slow evolution of life through long geologic ages. Geologic time, the record of fossils, and stratigraphy are all based on observational evidence—they are by no means hypothetical—and even if we went no further they are sufficient to demolish the creationist views about the dating of Creation, about past life on earth, and Noah's Flood. The geologic time scale was in fact established by geologists who were creationists, in keeping with their times, nearly two decades before the publication of Darwin's book on evolution. It is interesting to note that the time scale and the world stratigraphic system (both attacked by the creationists) are tested and corroborated every time an oil well is drilled through a predictable sequence of strata.

In all these arguments the creationists believe that if the Bible is not considered as literal truth, then its moral and ethical teachings are also invalid. Liberal and educated Christians, Jews, and Muslims, on the other hand, have no difficulty regarding the Bible as allegorical and symbolic, and yet they derive from it great spiritual and moral lessons (Frye, 1983). They, and this would include people from all walks of life, including many scientists, would agree with St. Augustine that God is everywhere, God *is* the entire cosmos; His center is everywhere and His periphery nowhere.

Every Bible reader is well aware that many biblical stories are difficult and obscure, requiring free interpretation, both in translating them and in thinking about them. Recently Robert Alter, in *The Art of Biblical Narrative,* has carefully summarized modern analyses of the old Hebrew Bible. This is a thought-provoking work which brings out the many contradictions and difficulties encountered in accepting every verse of Genesis as unassailably accurate.

During times of stress such as the present many people turn to religion, even pseudoreligion, for comfort. The two decades from 1960 to 1980 saw an astonishing multiplication of new cults and a significant growth of fundamentalism in America. Orthodox religious people usually accept instruction from their leaders who thereby derive prestige and authority as God's spokesmen, but history shows that these leaders are not uniformly wise in their use of this power. One has only to recall American Puritans and the Spanish Inquisition.

Finally I should like to define the word science, and explain why scientific creationism cannot be included in its definition. Science is characterized by the willingness of an investigator to follow evidence wherever it leads. It rests on testable observations and natural processes continuously moving ahead with new evidence and new viewpoints. It is, of necessity, self-correcting.

On the other hand, the "proofs" of the creationists consist not of testable observations, or analysis of the basic processes of creation, but of attacks on scientists and their methods. Dr. Duane Gish, a leading spokesman for the creationists, says: "We do not know how God created, what processes He used, *for God used processes which are not now operating anywhere in the natural universe*" (*Evolution—The Fossils Say No!*, 1973). When creationists speak in this manner they are not thinking as scientists and their religious beliefs should not be labeled science.

Creationism has not been revised or altered since the Book of Genesis was composed by primitive tribesmen more than 2,700 years ago. It served well for them because they had no scientific knowledge about natural causes, but it does not serve today as a reliable guide to the history or the nature of the universe.

The sciences concerned with the past can determine much of what happened long ago: how, where, and when events occurred. But they cannot discover the purpose or destiny of human existence. These ideas lie in the mind of each individual—and are the domain of religion, morality, and philosophy. Science cannot, and does not, pretend that it will ever be able to answer all the questions of life.

I am grateful to the scholars whose judgments I have sought during the writing of this volume: Niles Eldredge, Bobb Schaeffer, and John Lee of the American Museum of Natural History; Robert Guernsey, physicist with the IBM Corporation; Bentley Glass, biologist and professor emeritus of the New York State University at Stony Brook; and John Purcell, a member of the editorial board of *Scientific American*. Dr. Ruth Nanda Anshen read and discussed with me the entire manuscript. She edited and saw the first edition through publication. I am grateful for her encouragement and help. Manuel Guedes, artist, prepared most of the drawings and charts, and Elisabeth de Picciotto assisted him in their completion. Finally I thank my wife, Gillian, who engaged me in loving debate over every paragraph and comma. Of course she and the other cooperative consultants are not responsible for my views. In the last analysis I had to make my own decisions.

1

Patterns of Life

Knowledge and teaching are natural to human society. This is because man, who shares with the other animals such animal traits as sensation, movement, and the need for food and shelter, is distinguished from them by his ability to think. [Ibn Khaldun of Tunis, *Prolegomena*, ca. 1375.]

If the Lord Almighty had consulted me before embarking upon the Creation, I should have recommended something simpler. [Alphonso the Wise of Castile and León, ca. 1250.]

The Present Scene

I live on the Hudson River Palisades, which lie in a beautiful yet densely populated and altered area. Through the wisdom and generosity of John D. Rockefeller, Jr., a narrow belt of reclaimed woodland along the Palisades has been preserved for public enjoyment as the Palisades Interstate Park. This is a wildlife sanctuary overlooking New York City across the river. In this improbable location there remains only a poor relict of what was once a mighty hardwood forest, but it is nonetheless a useful and instructive example of the woodland environment scattered around the world. Natural order is plainly shown in the wondrous cycle of birth, growth, death, and rebirth, as in any forest biome or, for that matter, any natural assemblage of organisms.

The individual populations of the species of plants and animals that live together here form an ecological community, and the many species are linked together in mutual relationships, each with its unique environmental role.

Every plant species, in its own way, manufactures food and liberates oxygen by photosynthesis. Part of the energy, stored

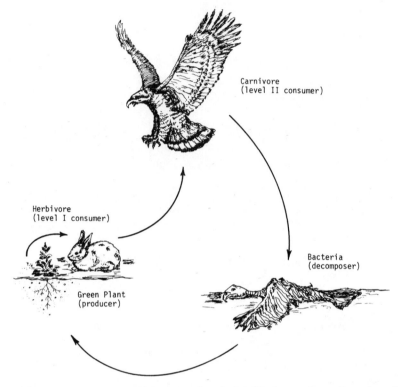

Figure 1.1. Energy cycle in a species chain. (Redrawn from Francisco J. Ayala and James W. Valentine.)

chemically from sunlight, is carried in falling leaves and other litter to the humus below. Browsing deer feed on foliage, bark, twigs, and buds; insects, slugs, and snails feed on plant juices and gnaw leaves and roots. Squirrels and mice collect acorns and seeds, many of which are buried in the ground for safe keeping and are then frequently forgotten to sprout later in the spring. Predators—dogs, cats, and hawks—eat the plant-eaters.

When the plants and animals die and are consumed by scavengers, the cycle is completed, always with a tremendous loss in energy and bulk at each successive level in the food pyramid.

Nutrients are returned to the soil where they are again available to the plants. The decaying litter is churned into the ground and mixed with mineral grains by frost, birds, rodents, spiders, insects, and worms—a continuous tilling of the soil—while decomposition by the weather, bacteria, fungi, beetles, ants, and termites, is in full swing.

From the surface of the ground downward to a depth of several meters there exists a concealed world of organisms, ranging from small to microscopic, living in burrows and throughout the aerated soil. Many of the principal groups of animals that live above ground are also represented here along with the soil-making and nitrogen-fixing microbes. The crucial importance of the soil community becomes apparent if we note that it supplies nutrients on a vast scale for the organisms above ground and the adjacent marine habitats of the continental margins. In both temperate and tropical soils organisms can be as diverse and abundant as the surface life; a handful of humus may contain billions of individuals from hundreds of species.

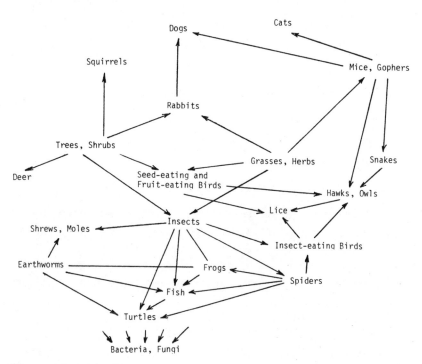

Figure 1.2. Web of interdependence. The success or failure of any species affects others.

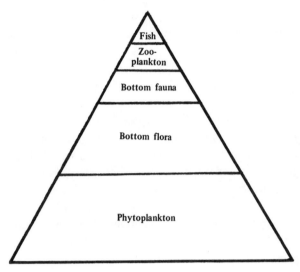

Figure 1.3. Productivity of a Wisconsin lake. The upward decrease in biomass and energy in any food chain is characteristic of all ecologic systems. (After C. Juday. *Wisconsin Lakes.* Wisconsin Academy of Sciences, vol. 34, 1943.)

The life of the forest pulsates with a rhythm of activity and change. Each organism makes its own contribution to the transmission of energy from sunlight and its distribution throughout the biosphere. Here is neither chaos nor perfect order. What order there is seems to be maintained by interactions, a symbiosis between organisms and their particular surroundings, a continuous recycling of materials and chemical energy among the organisms and their environmental reservoirs kept recharged by sunlight.

Nothing is static here; yesterday things were different and the changes that we see taking place guarantee that tomorrow will not be like today. Relationships and configurations change with time and cannot be exactly repeated. This seems to be the normal course of the history of life.

What is the source of this machinelike impersonal activity? Studies by many generations of experts in field and laboratory indicate that biological systems are products of the interdependence and adjustments that result in a delicate balance between organisms and their environments. The flexibility with which accommodations are made to changes lies in the marked tendency of life forms to vary, and through their variation they are able to take advantage of opportunities to reduce stress. When the biological accommodations become fixed in heredity, we say that evolution has taken place.

The Past

For the 2 million or so annual visitors to New York's American Museum of Natural History, where I have spent most of my career, an introduction to the scientific history of the universe is an exciting experience. For them, especially the schoolchildren, the fossil skeletons of great dinosaurs and other extinct creatures, and the grandeur of the Hayden Planetarium provide dramatic evidence that the universe has changed—clearly it has not always been as we now find it. It is evident that the present world is a result of a long and complex history. The visitor's curiosity is aroused and the experience opens a door to undreamed of marvels.

I like the comment by Walter Sullivan, science editor of the *New York Times*: "Curiosity is an essential ingredient of successful intelligence. We see it, in ways that delight us, in our small mammalian friends as they go sniffing about. We know that it is the kernel of science. . . . If curiosity dies, it would seem that intelligence is likely to do so, as well."

How can the highlights of past events and scenes be reconstructed and dated when there was no one to observe and record them? What are the scientific principles employed? The answers to these questions form fascinating chapters in the making of the earth, with profound significance in shaping man's attitude toward himself and the universe.

Paleontology, the study of fossils, is an evolutionary science that concerns itself with answering questions about the remains of past life entombed in the rocks. What was that organism? How old is it? Where and how did it live and die? Who were its ancestors and descendants? What does it tell us about past environments and the history of life?

Geology and biology, linked with paleontology, provide perspective and understanding of the origins and history of both man and his earth. These sciences are readily understandable and perhaps more rewarding to the nontechnical person than the more frequently studied physics and chemistry.

Expert paleontologists read chronological sequences of fossils on a worldwide scale much the same way that musicians read a musical score. To carry the analogy further, paleontologists also identify separate divisions and passages of the standard geological time scale with local variations on the score. Government geological organizations, oceanographic institutions, and petroleum companies employ teams of paleontologists for this activity. They read the fossil record from top to bottom through thousands of meters of crustal strata and they know from the accumulated experience of nearly two centuries that the standard time sequence of fossils is approximately the same the world over.

In paleontology and geology even the most elementary understanding of scientific evidence opens doors to exciting trips of exploration through time, both real and vicarious. To me and many other paleontologists the interpretation of fossils is infinitely fascinating, and the world of fossils provides adventures of the spirit comparable to the enjoyment of fine literature, art, and music.

Points of View

A very large part of the general public still equates evolution with the monkey-to-man parody instead of the scientific view of great and persistent changes in nature—changes in life, the earth, and the entire universe. Some people still suffer the Victorian sense of outrage and disbelief at the proposition that man is part of nature and not created in *their* image of God. No other contribution of science has so distressed conservative religious people as has organic evolution.

The conflict arises, I think, because naturalistic explanations of the origins of the universe, life, and humanity are thought by many to dispense with the metaphysical tenets of theology. In

Figure 1.4. Michelangelo's *Creation of Adam*, symbol of the Ages. (Sistine Chapel, Vatican City, Rome.)

large part, the emotional distaste for evolution stems from a lack of understanding of the respective roles of science and religion. Even among Christians, there is a spectrum of ideas about God. Religious evolutionists might well say that their God is the God of nature who carries out His work by strictly natural means, not by elusive, unpredictable, ad hoc miracles which cannot be subjected to critical examination.

Science is based on skepticism and irreverence for authority and tradition. It rejects the certainty of fundamentalism. Scientific explanations are based on experience, analogy, and objective testing, with expectation of revision to accommodate new information and new ways of looking at things. Religious canons traditionally demand unhesitating acceptance of church tradition and theological wisdom without tests or revision. The conflict is likely to continue as long as people are not willing to adapt their religious beliefs to secular knowledge about the real world.

Of course, scientific knowledge does not illuminate all aspects of human experience. The intangible values of the quality of life, beauty, spirituality, taste, inspiration, and imagination have proved to be intractable to scientific analysis; for human values, while real, are not fixed and universal. They change with time and place, and with breadth and depth of understanding. Beauty lies in the eyes of the beholder, but it also increases with understanding.

Harlow Shapley, the great Harvard astronomer, once observed

in *Beyond the Observatory* (1967) that there is spiritual wealth in nature and that to be a participant is in itself a glory. "With our fellow animals and plants of land, air, and sea, the rocks and waters of the earth, and the photons and atoms that make up the stars; with all these we are associated in an existence and an evolution that inspires respect and reverence." Shapley is right. We cannot escape humility, and as groping philosophers and scientists we are thankful for the mysteries that lie beyond our grasp.

Now, let us turn to the creationists. Who are they and what do they want? Why have they been accorded a wide hearing among educated people?

2

Trouble in Eden

The heart of both religion and science is adherence
to a body of law, indeed, the *same* body of law, that can
be referred to by one as the Word of God, by the other
as Natural Law. [Hobart W. Smith, *The Biologist.* February 1973, p. 24.]

It is only in the Bible that we can possibly obtain any information about the methods of creation, the order of creation, the duration of creation, or any other details of creation. [Henry M. Morris, *Remarkable Birth of Planet Earth.* Institute for Creation Research, San Diego, February 1972.]*

The Controversy

In 1896, when Andrew Dickson White, diplomat and first
president of Cornell University, published his definitive two-volume work, *A History of the Warfare of Science With Theology in Christendom*, he thought that the old conflict between religious conservatives and scientists was over. He said, "the theory of an evolutionary process in the formation of the universe and of animated nature is established, and the old theory of direct creation is gone forever . . . Science has given us conceptions far more noble, and opened the way to an argument for design infinitely more beautiful than any ever developed by theology."

White was woefully wrong about the war being over, and there is no evidence that his monumental history had the slightest influence on antievolutionists. Americans were astounded to discover, in 1925, that the conflict had not subsided. In that year the

* The italics found in the quotations at the beginning of this and the following chapters are the author's. They are inserted in order to emphasize the sources of creationist arguments.

state of Tennessee passed a law prohibiting the teaching of evolution and a test of that law was promptly organized by the American Civil Liberties Union. John Thomas Scopes, a public schoolteacher, agreed to make the test; he was convicted on his own admission and fined. It was one of the most widely publicized trials in history. William Jennings Bryan, three times Democratic nominee for the presidency of the United States and one time Secretary of State, assisted the prosecution. Clarence Darrow, the most famous civil rights lawyer of his time, aided the defense. The trial, which attracted worldwide attention, is entertainingly recounted in Irving Stone's *Clarence Darrow for the Defense.* Darrow's view: "Scopes isn't on trial; civilization is on trial. The prosecution is opening the doors for a reign of bigotry equal to anything in the Middle Ages. No man's belief will be safe if they win." Bryan: "The trial uncovers an attack for a generation on revealed religion. A successful attack would destroy the Bible and with it revealed religion. If evolution wins Christianity goes."

The two men, celebrated orators skilled at manipulating public emotions, debated "the Rock of Ages versus the age of the Rocks," but the Tennessee law stayed in effect for forty years before it was declared unconstitutional by the U.S. Supreme Court, and repealed.

Since those days most Americans have assumed that a secure victory for evolution had been won because of Bryan's pathetic performance. Not so! The Scopes affair and the emotions that it aroused among religious conservatives so intimidated textbook publishers and school officials throughout the country that evolution disappeared from most school systems and from many colleges. Antievolution really won the battle. As Irving Stone wrote, "As long as mankind inhabits this earth, no issue, no matter how cruel, stupid, vicious, or destructive, is ever dead."

The Scientific Creationists

In the late 1950s science teachers, dissatisfied with the poor quality of biology textbooks, organized a writer's group of the leading biologists, the Biological Sciences Curriculum Study (BSCS), which prepared and published several trial editions of biology books for use in high schools. Religious fundamentalists, calling themselves scientific creationists, and still preaching the evils of nineteenth-century Darwinism, immediately went on the offensive, although well aware that evolutionary principles—the scientific mechanisms of change—have come to form the basis of all science which is dynamic, not static: astronomy, physics, chemistry, geology, biology, and the social sciences. The creationist revolt is not simply an emotional revulsion against man's animal connections. It is an anguished protest against the whole cosmology of science and many other aspects of modernity.

The creationists' answer to the uncertainties of a modern technological society is to purge education of knowledge that seems to conflict with their fundamentalist beliefs, and they would like to change all society to conform with their ultra-conservative doctrine. This, of course, is a contradiction in objectives because an advanced technology is impossible without a constantly pioneering, free, basic science.

In 1963 the Creation Research Society was organized as a national scientific society with headquarters in Ann Arbor, Michigan. Its objective was to gain widespread acceptance of the biblical version of special Creation as being historical truth supported by scientific evidence. The members called themselves scientific creationists, and the society grew to between five and six hundred full members in the late 1970s. Voting members must subscribe to the society's credo which states, in part, that the account of origins in Genesis is a factual representation of simple historical truths. All basic types of living things, including man, were made by direct creative acts of God during Creation week. . . . Whatever biological changes have occurred since Creation have been only within the original created kinds. The Noachian Deluge was an historical event, worldwide in its extent and effect.

The society has its own quarterly journal in which it publishes progress in the search for evidence to support biblical Creation and to discredit evolution. In addition, the society has its own biology textbook for high schools from which evolutionary heresy has been purged: *Biology: A Search for Order in Complexity.*

Affiliated educational organizations take their cues from headquarters in Ann Arbor and San Diego. Branches over the country have such names as Bible-Science Association, Creation Science Research Center, Creation Science and Humanities Society, Students for Origins Research, Educational Research Analysts, Boosters of True Education, and many others.

Ambassador College, a Bible school of the Worldwide Church of God, with campuses in Pasadena, California and Big Sandy, Texas, publishes and distributes antievolution literature to school children. Former president of the college, Garner Ted Armstrong, charismatic television evangelist, says in his *Some Fishy Stories About Evolution*: "Believe it or not, evolution is one of the greatest HOAXES ever foisted off on an unsuspecting world and it has come to deeply *permeate* the whole of modern education, and with it, society."

The Jehovah's Witnesses (Watchtower Bible and Trust Society) published a small book, *Did We Get Here by Evolution or by Creation?*, in 1967. By the early 1970s more than 14 million copies of this book had been printed and translated into eleven languages, according to the publisher. This extraordinary effort is clear evidence of an immense commitment.

The chief center of antievolution acitivity unquestionably is the Institute for Creation Research, a division of the Christian Heritage College in San Diego. Through its Creation-Life Publishers, it provides a steady flow of antievolution literature from the fertile pens and imaginations of a dozen or so creationists. The "research" literature consists of original essays and innumerable critiques of the literature on evolution. Especially emphasized are innumerable quotations from the published works of leading scientists. These quotations are given out of context, carefully selected to demonstrate disagreements and confusion among evolutionists. In this way arguments are built against evolution but the reader is not told what the evolutionists are arguing about. Instead, he is left with the erroneous impression that evolution itself is under attack. Actually, the differences pertain to technical details about the mechanisms of evolution which would not be understood by a lay reader. The consensus among evolutionists is that evolution is a universal fact of nature.

Creation-Life Publishers distributes cassettes, filmstrips, and "documentary" movies on how creationists discovered human footprints in association with dinosaur tracks at Glen Rose, Texas, and other investigations on alleged remains of the Ark on Mount Ararat. They also sponsor radio and television programs and publish monthly newsletters (*Acts & Facts* and *Impact*).

The Institute For Creation Research promotes public debates with university scientists around the country, almost certainly their most effective manner of obtaining the attention of nonfundamentalist audiences. In these debates, the scientists are at a disadvantage and frequently do not make a good showing. The reasons are clear. The creationists insist that all reference to religion and the Bible be excluded from the debates and they freely attack the foundations of science with their own brand of pseudoscience, while the evolutionists try to make a defense in terms understandable to nonscientific audiences. The creationists are poised and impressively self-confident from hundreds of hours of combat while the scientists are trained to stress the uncertainties characteristic of all science. The debates are heavily attended by religious conservatives who provide an enthusiastic claque for the creationists.

Dorothy Nelkin, Cornell University's expert on public disputes, says in the April 1976 *Scientific American*:

> The suggestion that questions of scientific fact and scientific education should be settled by public debate has left most scientists amazed. Would the lay community really want to give quack doctors equal time with licensed doctors? . . . Would the community entertain putting a paragraph in the Book of Genesis to indicate that the scientific method rejects supernatural explanations of the universe? . . . Scientific concepts are taught when they are generally accepted by the scientific community. In fact, it is precisely that acceptance by the scientific community that acts to validate one concept and reject another; acceptance by those outside the scientific community is irrelevant.

A panel of twenty-one writers and consultants of the Institute has issued a book for general distribution to public school teachers under the title *Scientific Creationism*, edited by Henry M. Morris. This instructs teachers how to avoid references to religion and the Bible in presenting creationist arguments in the classroom and how to challenge the geological and biological sciences with respect to the antiquity of the earth and organic evolution. None of the contributors is noted for original scientific contributions in the national journals, and their academic degrees would seem to have little direct bearing on evolution—engineering, biochemistry, general science, theology, physics, food technology, and creation research.

Legal Maneuvers

An early crest in antievolution sentiment occurred between 1922 and 1929 when fundamentalists declared war and introduced a flurry of legislation in thirty-seven states to banish evolution forever from the classroom. There was even talk of a constitutional amendment to prohibit teaching evolution. Three proposals at the state level were passed but were subsequently declared unconstitutional by the federal courts. Again, from the early 1960s until 1969, twenty-five new pieces of legislation, designed to discourage the teaching of evolutionary biology and to encourage creationism in the public schools, were submitted by creationists to state legislatures.

Attempts by creationists to mandate by law what is taught in science classes and what kinds of science should be supported by public funds probably will continue to be ineffectual short of a change in the Constitution. They are much more successful with their pressures on school boards, administrators, and teachers by making appeals for "fair play," "equal time," and "academic freedom" as, for example, in the city schools of Atlanta, Georgia, Cincinnati and Columbus, Ohio, and Columbia, South Carolina, and others, where students are exposed by complying teachers to both evolution and creationism in the same classes and are expected to draw their own conclusions or more frequently are kept in ignorance of the whole issue. Creationists deny that they are trying to bring the Bible into the science classroom. They say creationism is science and the fact that it has a religious foundation is quite accidental and irrelevant.

Even if this monstrous deception were acceptable, creationism and evolution are mutually antagonistic and cannot survive in the same classroom. Deprived by the Constitution of the opportunity to cite biblical authority in support of their views, the creationists have adopted an antiscience strategy. The contest or lack of contest in any classroom must depend on the integrity of the teacher and the weight of public opinion in the local community.

While the plea for equal time (or silence on the issue) in the classroom has been successful in some areas the underlying intention of the creationists is laid bare by remarks such as that of creationist James Velkamp, Professor of Education at Christian Heritage College: "We must be alert and resolute to bar from our classrooms all those in the bondage of humanism who question the inerrancy of the Bible, who doubt the literalness and historicity of the first chapters of Genesis . . . and who promulgate uniformitarian evolution . . ." (from a pamphlet—*Education for Eternity*, April 1979).

From time to time the San Diego creationists find "new evidence" (differences among evolutionists over evolutionary mechanisms) that reveals "major weaknesses" in evolutionary theory. Ronald Reagan, already indoctrinated by creationists while Governor of California, said to an evangelist gathering while he was campaigning in Texas for the presidential nomination: "I have a great many questions about evolution. I think that recent discoveries down through the years have pointed up great flaws in it." This is what the creationists would like the general public to believe, but nearly all research biologists and geologists are convinced that evolution is responsible for the diversity of life.

Textbook selection committees in every state are under pressure to adopt biology books that include favorable reference to divine Creation as biological science. Writers and publishers of these books are worried.

At present, nearly one half of the states have policies allowing local school boards to include creationism in their science classes if they wish. In other states the decision is left to state officials who are also vulnerable, and unwilling parents and students are always free to register formal complaints with the courts.

So far, the courts and legislatures in most states have been unsympathetic to creationism, which they correctly view as a ruse to circumvent the prohibition of pressing any particular religion in the public schools. However, in several states, creationism in some form has gained local footholds. In these places science teachers are intimidated. Obviously, court action is not the best way to restrain the creationists. Public opinion could be more effective.

The creationists attacked on a new front in 1978. The National Bible Knowledge Association and the National Foundation for Fairness in Education sued the Smithsonian Institution in U.S. District Court, hoping to stop work on a permanent exhibition of the principles of organic evolution. The plaintiffs contended that the Smithsonian was violating the government's role of religious neutrality as outlined in the First Amendment, by promoting a "religion of secular humanism." According to the *Washington Post* (December 12, 1978), the claim was rejected by U.S. District Court Judge Parker on the grounds that "The primary effect of the evolution exhibits is not to advance a religious theory or to inhibit plaintiffs in their religious beliefs. . . . The Supreme Court has made it clear that the state has no interest in protecting any of all religions from views distasteful to them."

Creationism is Not Science

Creationism cannot be defined as a science because it is based on an inflexible presupposition, a conviction based on supposed causes and events that cannot be examined either directly or indirectly by scientific methods. The conclusions precede the search for evidence. In addition, there is no scientific research into the basic tenets of creationism. Revelation is completely outside the scope of science. The "research" of creationists is a biased, destructive critique of all scientific investigation of origins. The basic position of creationism is negative, that is, creationists seek to enhance their credibility by destroying the opponent, not by building their own case.

Creationists have found that some people will accept their statements if they are made enough times with the right emphasis and solemnity. Typical examples: "Evolution cannot be proved, it is one-sided and dogmantic and should be countered by alternative explanations of man's background. This is essential to good pedagogy." "Many scientists are disillusioned with evolutionary explanations and have found creationism preferable and since special Creation is the only alternative to evolution it should be given more attention in public school curricula." "The creationist model better explains the fossil record and many geological phenomena than does evolutionary theory." "The 'gospel' of evolution is the enemy of the Gospel of Christ and the problem of origins is simply incapable of solution by scientific means."

All of these statements, which have acquired the status of slogans, are irresponsible and patently false.

Scientists Divided

The sterile controversy over evolution is not, as the creationists would like the public to believe, a split within the scientific community, because the creationists are not part of that community. They have isolated themselves even though some have advanced science training. They are religious activists who, for the most part, are engaged as part-time evangelists, teachers, and engineers. They wield disproportionate influence simply because they are organized and powerfully motivated in a common cause.

When science has split the atom, cracked the genetic code, and put men on the moon, the efforts of creationists to turn back the clock has an eerie quality. They are not barefoot hill folk, but they are suspicious of science and higher education and are very much in earnest in their compulsion to take science education into their own hands. They are winning converts to their ranks.

Misuse of the Bible

In their war on evolutionary science, creationists use the Bible as a symbol, a rallying point calculated to win sympathy and to enhance their influence among religious conservatives.

The Bible has shaped Western civilization and it unquestionably is the most influential book of all time. It is not, however, a substitute for secular learning. Unreasoning insistence on a "literal" interpretation of all biblical statements inevitably leads to endless conflicts between reason and blind acceptance—a flat earth at the center of the universe, fewer ribs in men than in women, a fantasy about a universal flood and a magical Ark commodious enough to salvage all terrestrial plants and animals and all the life of fresh waters which cannot endure even brief immersion in sea water. (Isaac Asimov discusses this problem at length in his scholarly *In the Beginning*, published in New York, 1981.)

Henry M. Morris, Director of the Institute for Creation Research, self-appointed spokesman for creationists everywhere, voices a self-defeating, all-or-nothing view in his *Biblical Catastrophism and Geology* (1974 pamphlet) that must turn many thoughtful young people away from the great moral lessons of the Bible:

Pious veneration of the Bible for its "spiritual" values is hardly consistent with a rejection of its scientific and historical teachings, for if the latter cannot be trusted—that is, statements which are susceptible to actual human investigation and proof—then how can its "spiritual" teachings, which are not susceptible of proof, be trusted?

Great writers have always made use of metaphor and allegory in bringing together thoughts and images as an effective way to impress ideas in the minds of people. The Bible, in common with all great literature, makes use of metaphor, allegory, and other poetic devices. Theologians have interpreted biblical metaphor and allegory in many different ways; rarely have they regarded it as a font of literal truth or as being equivalent to science.

The principles of the Bible are not diminished if we recognize that the Scriptures originated as oral traditions among Middle Eastern tribes, and have been compiled, transcribed, and translated into most of the world's languages by countless fallible human scribes. Today, thoughtful Bible readers must choose between interpreting the several versions of the Scriptures freely, according to their own consciences and level of comprehension, or they must accept some ecclesiastical authority. The creationists are on the side of those churches that frown on free interpretation of the Bible.

The Causes of Controversy

How is it that a handful of extremist American evangelicals preaching a repressive doctrine have been able to challenge modern science and to polarize communities into resentful factions for or against bringing creationism into the public schools? Their success is the more astonishing because creationists freely admit that most of the world's scientists accept evolution as a well-established principle of nature.

In her book, *Science Textbook Controversies and the Politics of Equal Time,* Dorothy Nelkin stresses the failure of science and technology to live up to the aspirations of the American dream. Antievolutionists hold science responsible for the disintegration of spiritual and moral values and the deterioration of the environment. They feel that the only conceivable remedy to the worsening alienation must be to return to the values of truth and moral certainty of a more innocent age.

In the past, there has always been some resistance to science and intellectualism, but in Nelkin's view modern Americans are confused and ambivalent about what they want. She cites public opinion polls that show an overwhelming majority to be convinced that science is necessary for a high standard of living, while almost as many believe that we are too dependent on science. In any case, she concludes that the present antievolution campaign is a backlash against science and the intrusion of government in education.

Other factors should be considered. Evangelical people, numbering perhaps as many as 20 percent of our population, believe that they must show others their particular route to salvation. And they naturally are pleased with the misconceived idea that something called "science" does, indeed, support their religious convictions. They can be counted on to favor any cause that is said to be a defense of the Bible. They are vulnerable to the message of the creationists who charge that the aspects of science that deal with the origin of mankind are destructive to morality and a threat to religious values. Traditionally, fundamentalists have always rejected the idea that man is an animal. Thomas H. Huxley, great nineteenth-century biologist, concluded that they were "alarmed lest man's moral nature be debased by the increase of his knowledge."

Scientists and science are sometimes erroneously identified with, and even held responsible for, warfare and the many unwanted consequences of modern technology. However, many of these are direct results of industrial development and runaway population growth, and to solve or ameliorate them we need more science, not less.

Finally, there has always been a suspicion that scientists as a group are atheists or worse. I suspect that there are no more atheists among scientists than in any other group of people. Religious scientists could well argue that the most direct route to God is through his works—the study of natural constructions and the natural forces that make them rather than the metaphysical conventions and legends of formal religion.

Herein lies the vast gap between creationism and science. The former is based on the presupposition that biblical revelation is the highest form of truth and that anything that does not agree with, or seems to disagree with, the Scriptures is by definition false. The fascinating patterns of nature are "explained" by creationists as ideas in the mind of God at the time of the Creation of the universe. No research is possible in that direction, either by creationists or scientists.

On the other hand, the authentic scientist does not regard revealed truth as reliable. Instead, the striking regularities that he finds in nature capture his interest and demand inquiry. He is especially interested in learning about the meaning of those regularities, how they came into being and how they are sustained. If they are the expression of "God's will," so be it. But how does nature carry out "God's will?" That is the business of science.

Scientists place their faith in the amazing potential of the human intellect. Thousands of years of human history have taught scholars to be wary of knowledge that stems solely from tradition and authority. Scientists regard scientific truth as a goal to be sought but they think it unlikely that total truth is attainable.

On the other hand, creationism does not resemble science; it is a militant theology of a particularly uncompromising and narrow kind that foments discord. The efforts of the creationists are sadly misdirected. The proper field of concern of their religion should be morality and spirituality, not the nature, origin, and history of the universe. These matters belong to science. At a time when our future, indeed our very survival, demands clear understanding of science and its methods, the creationists are taking steps which, if successful, surely would cripple our scientific effort.

In the United States of America people with—or without— religious faith have every right to speak as citizens and they also have the citizen's right to be wrong. The creationists menace religious and intellectual freedom, however, when they try to make their views binding on others. Ours is a society of many faiths. As the architects of our Constitution brilliantly recognized, no one's God is sovereign in the United States.

It is an interesting and negative aspect of religion that so many people in the world have received God's message only to quarrel with each other about the meaning of that message. Most scientists take the position that God is a power beyond understanding and that to profess intimate knowledge of Him is an act devoid of humility.

How does it happen that so many people with a comparatively high level of education are today unable to distinguish between fantasy and reality? Let's examine this disturbing situation in the next chapter.

3

Fantasy and Reality

The past teemed with unknown gods who visited the primeval earth in manned spaceships. [Erich von Däniken, *Chariots of the Gods?* New York: Putnam's, 1971.]

A human-like sandal print with several trilobites in it near Delta, Utah. . . . Another spectacular find: giant men's footprints* in the same bed with dinosaur and brontosaurus tracks. Clearly man and the dinosaur lived at the same time. [John N. Moore and Harold Schultz Slusher, ed., *Biology: A Search for Order in Complexity.* A textbook of the Creation Research Society.]

Scientific Illiteracy

Learning about the ancient history of life is purely a scientific problem. Since our present society is based on scientific technology, it might be assumed that educated people of an industrialized nation such as the United States would be well informed about the nature and significance of scientific evidence and the high standards demanded by modern science. Clearly this is not so. People with little or no elementary scientific training who are not acquainted with the essential nature of science make up a large part of the general public. They cherish the factual, love the imaginative, but do not know the difference between the two. Consequently, they are susceptible to error when presented with problems that require for their solution at least elementary scientific knowledge—knowledge of the limitations, as well as the potentials, of science.

---

* I have examined these prints along the Paluxey River, near Glen Rose, Texas. Only eyes deceived by fond expectation could interpret them as human footprints. They include badly corroded dinosaur prints and gravel-scoured oval pits eroded in bedrock by the river.

It is natural to be attracted by the mysterious and the sensational, even when they are recognized as being doubtful. Consequently, it is not surprising that people who prefer emotional stimulation to analytical thought frequently turn to hallucinogens, mysticism, and religious cults—psychological crutches that replace self-discipline, responsibility, and rational doubt.

The current exaggerated interest in astrology, the occult, monsters, creationism, and visitors from outer space is a mass renunciation of mature reason, since these topics are deficient in both theory and evidence.

Beliefs termed "supernatural" need not be wholly without validity. In some cases they may embrace real phenomena that are at present not objectively supportable. In other cases they are demonstrably absurd. In any event, they seem to be based on fanciful rather than rational causes. The occult seems to give people moral direction, a group affiliation, and profound feelings of fear and pleasure. The occult also seems to engender belief systems that characteristically invite total commitment from their members (e.g., scientology, theosophy, Satanism, UFO cults, and extremist pseudoreligions).

Edward Gibbon, in his great *The History of the Decline and Fall of the Roman Empire,* published in 1776, attributed the extraordinary rejection of reality in the Middle Ages to the triumph of religious superstition. "How shall we excuse the supine inattention," he asks,

to those evidences which were presented by the hand of Omnipotence, not to their reason but to their senses? During the age of Christ, of his Apostles, and of their first disciples, the doctrine which they preached was confirmed by innumerable prodigies. The lame walked, the blind saw, the sick were healed, daemons expelled, and the laws of nature were frequently suspended for the benefit of the Church ... the frequent instances ... were extremely convenient for the purpose of removing every difficulty, and of silencing every objection. The most extravagent legends were applauded by the credulous multitude, countenanced by the power of the clergy and attested by the suspicious evidence of ecclesiastical history.

Gibbon saw the Christian miracles as a strategy for gaining a following and securing a righteous end.

Appalled by a growing sense of superstition in America, a group of distinguished scholars headed by Paul Kurtz, philosophy professor at the State University of New York at Buffalo, have formed a Committee for the Scientific Investigation of Claims of the Paranormal (CSICP). They publish *The Skeptical Inquirer*, a journal designed to help the public distinguish between fact and fiction. This committee, including such a public figure as Isaac Asimov, is solidly opposed to the commercial and ideological exploitation of the public.

Pseudoscience

One manifestation of general naiveté in scientific matters is a growing phenomenon known as pseudoscience, of which creationism is an example. Pseudoscience is characterized by sensational claims of exciting new discoveries. Conclusions supported by little corroboration are announced that run counter to hard-won scientific knowledge. The aficionados of pseudoscience say that the scientific "establishment" is dominated by ultraconservative leaders, hostile to new ideas and jealous of their positions. However, nobody likes to think that he or she is being deliberately misled and there is frequently an embarrassed retreat when the truth is recognized.

The purpose of scientific literature is to report and explain impartially. Pseudoscientific literature, on the other hand, misinforms and confuses. It is sensational speculation irresponsibly marketed as serious science, and it lacks the essential characteristics of science in several respects. Chief among these is misuse and distortion of evidence in support of fixed ideas coupled with intolerance of conflicting observations. The primary objective is validation of a claim, not an impartial search for the truth. Solemn repetition of groundless assertions takes the place of critical, impartial analysis of evidence.

Pseudoscience differs from science fiction in that it is designated by authors and publishers as nonfiction. Pseudoscience leans heavily on the supernatural and other ad hoc imagined causes contrived to entertain, excite, or alarm the reader.

*"That's the gist of what I want to say. Now get
me some statistics to base it on."*

Figure 3.1. Pseudoscience: manipulation of evidence to support a fixed
idea. Drawing by Joe Mirachi; © 1977 The New Yorker Magazine, Inc.

The Velikovsky Cult

The current wave of popular interest in pseudoscience extends
back to the 1950s when two book-length sensational fantasies on
earth history, *Worlds in Collision* and *Earth in Upheaval,* published
by Immanuel Velikovsky, a professional psychiatrist and amateur
historian, attracted wide attention. He became a cause célèbre with
the general public and a symbol for an antiscience cult when the
scientific press refused to publish his ideas, which they regarded
not as science but as mysticism and amateur speculation. Velikovsky
was then forced to turn to the popular press for support.

His hypothesis was based on two highly improbable assumptions: (1) that he could identify worldwide catastrophes in both prehistorical and historical times, and (2) that these catastrophes were caused by mysterious movements of the planets Venus and Mars. Velikovsky's sources consisted of the Bible and other ancient documents, myths, legends, and archaeological and geological data generally selected out of context and excluding information that did not harmonize with his presuppositions. How is an uninformed public to decide whether such an innovator is mentally flawed or a genius? He is criticized by scientists not because his ideas are unorthodox or because they pose a threat to widely accepted views, as claimed by his credulous admirers, but because he and his publishers present his books as serious science, long after their scientific worth has been rejected by a whole generation of experts.

The community of scientists, like any democratic institution, cannot long be authoritarian. It encompasses too wide a range of diverse individuals in universities, institutes, museums, government, and industrial research laboratories, as well as university students carrying out original scientific research as part of their training. If we look over this list these people have little in common beyond their search for knowledge. In some respects they are competitors. Science thrives on dissent and intramural criticism.

The Velikovsky issue has revealed the disturbing extent to which the public is unable to form unemotional judgments about questions involving scientific evidence. People so often appear to be more interested in controversy in the ranks of scientists than in the merits of the differences. Considering the overwhelming scientific evidence, there should never have been a Velikovsky affair, but new cult organizations and publications (e.g., *Kronos*, a periodical published at Glassboro State College, New Jersey) devoted mainly to his adulation are still appearing in this country and abroad. Velikovskyism as a significant episode in American science has been well analyzed recently by Donald Goldsmith and a panel of leading scientists in *Scientists Confront Velikovsky*.

Devils and Gods

Other spectacularly successful examples of pseudoscientific literature are *The Bermuda Triangle*, by Charles Berlitz, and *Chariots of the Gods?* by Erich von Däniken. Few authentic works of science have ever been as popular!

In the first, Berlitz speculates about the "mysterious" disappearances of airplanes and ships in the Atlantic north of Puerto Rico. Since causes of many of the disappearances are unknown, the author suggests extraterrestrial or supernatural agents. Lawrence Kusche has published an exposé based on careful research of the supposed mysteries in *The Bermuda Triangle Mystery—Solved.* He has no difficulty explaining the disappearances as conventional accidents in a region of exceptionally heavy traffic. According to Kusche, the supernatural or UFO explanation is simply "a copout of doing research—and a way to sell a lot of books." It is a sad comment on today's world that one of his students told him he hoped the mystery would *not* be solved, and that it would prove to be supernatural. Few admirers of Berlitz will be pleased with Kusche! Several more books on the Bermuda Triangle, quickly issued by other authors, took advantage of the bonanza.

First published in German in 1968, *Chariots of the Gods?* by Swiss writer Erich von Däniken was soon translated into English and taken up in 1971 for the American market as a paperback "nonfiction" book. By 1978 it had sold 35 million copies in scores of languages and was still near the top of the bestseller lists. Clearly, more is involved here than simple entertainment. Von Däniken cites archaeological mysteries in various parts of the world that confound the experts and then he proceeds to invent his own imaginative hypothesis that ancient stone structures and geometric designs on the ground in western South America, Egypt, and elsewhere, could not have been constructed by ancient man with primitive tools. *Therefore,* they must be the work of extraterrestrial creatures of advanced intellect.

The scientific community chose for several years to ignore von Däniken's story as too preposterous for comment. Finally, in 1976, Ronald Story published a well-documented refutation of von Däniken's fantasies and other UFO mythology in *The Space-Gods Revealed.* This book should be required reading for all high school students.

Ever since the sixteenth century, men have been employing scientific methods in an effort to detect and report supernatural phenomena, but the public will not relinquish its yearning for unsolvable mysteries. Scientists do not claim that they can solve all problems or explain all mysteries. Their experience shows that any appeal to unknown and unknowable causes has not been rewarding because it does not lead to truths about the universe. Reasonable skepticism, which should be a mark of education, frequently is discarded by people in favor of wishful thinking, self-delusion, and credulous superstition based, in no small measure, on the universal love of mystery for its own sake.

People of primitive cultures have commonly attributed the faculty of awareness to plants, but botanists find no basis for this idea. There are, indeed, many things about plant growth and behavior that are not yet well understood. For example, during growth plants respond delicately to the stimulation of light and gravity. Stems grow upward, branches diverge laterally, and roots grow downward. The ways in which plants respond to the daily and seasonal rhythms of sunlight are complex and involve little-understood mechanisms. Many kinds of blossoms twist their necks to follow the progress of the sun. Scientists do not have the slightest doubt that these responses follow laws of physics and chemistry, or that satisfactory and detailed explanations will eventually be forthcoming.

Cleve Backster, a lie detector expert, and his potted philodendron plant had a love affair in which it was said that the plant responded to changes in his thoughts and emotions. A 1973 bestseller, *The Secret Life of Plants*, describes the experience of Backster and others who attributed humanlike emotions and sensibilities to plants. The authors, Peter Tomkins and Christopher Bird, benefited from a preposterous advertising campaign and from several book club adoptions. Botanists have been unable to duplicate any of the experiments described in the book. Consequently, the scientific community gave no credence to the claims, but this did not prevent the public from eagerly and uncritically accepting them.

Arthur W. Galston, professor of botany at Yale University, wistfully observes in the Yale Alumni Magazine for December 1975, that many lay people, including university students, criticize as reactionary the disbelief of their botany professors. He thinks that the objective, rational way would be to withhold judgment:

"Until a reported phenomenon can be independently confirmed by critical researchers anywhere, it must not be accepted as true." Of course, the difficulty is that an untrained public does not understand scientific skepticism and frequently does not know how to recognize "critical researchers" or "independent confirmation."

A "documentary" commercial movie issued by the creationists covers alleged human footprints in direct association with dinosaur tracks near Glen Rose, Texas. Another describes various expeditions to Mount Ararat in search of Noah's Ark, which they are certain is preserved there.

Since they believe that the thick blanket of fossiliferous sedimentary rocks over the earth represents the deposits from the great Flood of Noah, it follows that the extinction of the dinosaurs, mammoths, and other great animals must have resulted from the rising flood waters as those animals tried to scramble to the highest places for safety.

Unhappily for their hypothesis, the fossil remains of these animals usually occur at low or intermediate elevations and they are not found where they should be, at the bottom of the sedimentary "Flood" deposits. Instead, they lie far above the base of the fossil record. For example, below the Glen Rose dinosaur footprints are about three kilometers of nearly flat sedimentary deposits as determined by deep borings for oil and by geophysical soundings.

The Importance of Understanding

Unusual or unfamiliar incidents frequently ignite a spark of superstition in people who then imagine unnatural and irrational explanations. Belief in magic and miracles has been part of human cultures since man acquired an imagination. This aspect of human nature teaches something about man's dreams and his psychological nature, but it does not provide any understanding of the concrete world. An educated person should be able to think for himself rather than passively accept the judgments of would-be leaders—to be able to recognize concealed self-interest and to make his own value judgments. Unthinking persons cannot choose for themselves but must let others choose for them. To fail to make one's own choice is to surrender freedom.

Experience shows that scientific methods have proved to be amazingly successful in explaining nature and emancipating mankind from the fear of the unknown. But the value of science goes further than this. It provides appreciation and an intellectual beauty that any intelligent and open-minded person can enjoy, and an order of reality that transcends the individual and his imagination. Many superficially unattractive phenomena become beautiful with understanding: we often hear computer analysts speak of *elegant* mathematical solutions to problems.

On hearing great music, many people are moved emotionally by a blend of voices and instruments—a kind of nonverbal language. If the listeners have a rudimentary understanding of rhythm, pitch, harmony, and acoustics, all of which are governed by the laws of physics, they enjoy an added dimension of experience. Intellectual beauty is then added to sensuous beauty. Only then is complete communication attained between composer and listener.

Some people feel uncomfortable with scientific advances, especially those discoveries that link man with nature, and they have a tendency to feel that "bad" knowledge should be suppressed. Walt Whitman, for example, charged that scientific analysis of nature somehow destroyed wonderment, making the universe less beautiful, and Keats denounced Newton for soiling the beauty of the rainbow by reducing it to its spectrum of colors. Even today there are eminent educators and politicians who display an appalling lack of appreciation of basic science, which they frequently confuse with engineering and technology.

Lewis Thomas, in *The Medusa and the Snail* (New York: Bantam Books, 1979, p. 59), expresses well the motivation of the scientist toward scientific knowledge.

Is there something fundamentally unnatural, or intrinsically wrong, or hazardous for the species, in the ambition that drives us all to reach a comprehensive understanding of nature, including ourselves? I cannot believe it. It would seem to me a more unnatural thing, and more of an offense against nature for us to come on the scene endowed as all human beings are with questions, and then for us to do nothing about it, or worse, to try to suppress the questions. . . . This, to my way of thinking is the real hubris, and it carries dangers for us all.

Theodore Roszak, a California State College historian, at Hayward, takes the opposite view. He savagely attacks reductionist science as creating a "monster of meaninglessness. The existential void where modern man searches in vain for his soul. . . . There is no experience of the divine, only the experience of man's infinite aloneness" (*Daedalus*, Summer 1974, p. 18). Clearly, Roszak does not understand the deeper meaning of science. It seems to me that his comment is equivalent to saying that ignorance of man's real place in the universe is better than knowledge leading to verifiable truth, that man was better off with his old superstitions and self-delusion about meaning and destiny. What we need is the merging of intuition and reason.

Clearly, each generation will develop its own ideas about these things, rejecting excessive constraints of the past. Let the critics quit looking for scapegoats and join in exploring this great and wonderful universe. Why is it that otherwise intelligent people will adopt a purely sentimental relationship with nature instead of seeking intellectual understanding and appreciation? I can only conclude that many would rather rely on imagination and sensuous enjoyment and that they do not place a high value on understanding.

To religious people who can contemplate nature with a measure of understanding there are transcendent rewards as hinted at in Wordsworth's *Tintern Abbey*:

And I have felt
A presence that disturbs me with the joy
Of elevated thoughts; a sense sublime
Of something far more deeply interfused,
Whose dwelling is the light of setting suns,
And the round ocean and the living air,
And the blue sky, and the mind of man.

4

Noah's Flood and Other Catastrophes

If we could behold in one view all the volcanic cones thrown up . . . during the last five thousand years, and could see the lavas which have flowed during the same period; the dislocations, subsidences, and elevations caused during earthquakes; the lands added to various deltas, or devoured by the sea, together with the effects of devastation by floods, and imagine that all these events had happened in one year, we must form most exalted ideas of the activity of the agents, and the suddenness of the revolutions. [Charles Lyell, *Principles of Geology.* London, 1860.]

If the universal Flood concept explains far better than other concepts many of the significant features of the earth's crust, why is it not more generally accepted by geologists? The answer, we feel, is twofold. In the first place, nothing less than a supernatural intervention could have caused such a Flood; and modern science, in the nature of the case, has no room whatsoever for such intervention. In the second place, the vast majority of historical geologists . . . can hardly qualify as competent and impartial judges in the matter. [John C. Whitcomb, Jr., creationist-theologian, *The World That Perished.*]

What Are Catastrophes?

Before the era of modern science, most people interpreted disasters as God's will, and some people still hold to this view. Plagues, floods, tempests, earthquakes, and volcanic eruptions were considered to be acts of an angry deity or evil spirits. The importance of such events was measured not by geologic changes in the landscape but by the level of terror, property damage, injuries, and deaths. Even today natural disasters are sometimes known as "Acts of God," a phrase still used in legal and insurance documents.

Many violent natural events are recurrent and are therefore relatively well understood; having natural causes they are relatively predictable. Whether or not they are considered rare or frequent is a matter of viewpoint and the time scale employed, commonly the life span or memory of eyewitnesses. A volcano that erupts

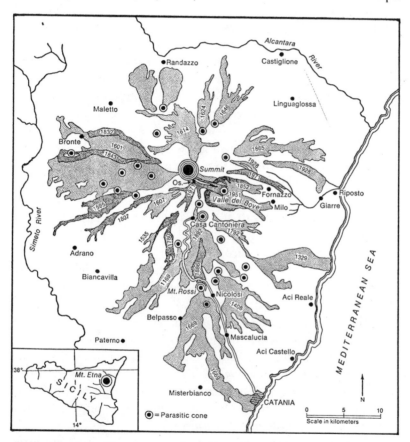

Figure 4.1. Mount Etna, Sicily. Eight centuries of frequent eruptions have made a negligible addition to the mountain mass. A single great explosion could destroy much of the accumulation of lava and ash. (Fred Bullard. *Volcanoes of the World*. Austin: University of Texas Press, 1978.)

only once or twice in a century would not be regarded as an imminent threat by a local villager, but it would be considered a frequent and dependable performer by a geologist.

Predictions of the timing and violence of a natural cataclysm usually must be only approximations, since such events are governed by complex and rapidly changing factors. Satellite photography, seismometers, laser recorders, and high-speed computers are aiding immeasurably in watching changes that are likely to become human hazards.

Naturalists in former times, citing the Scriptures as authority for a belief that the earth is very young, interpreted extinctions of ancient plants and animals and the deformation of rock layers as products of worldwide violent catastrophes early in the history of the earth. The causes were deemed to be unfathomable, probably miraculous. This concept, known as *catastrophism,* is still sustained by modern creationists. The issue is confused by the fact that the word "catastrophism" has also been revived recently by some geologists who make use of it in a very different sense to stress the fact that many ordinary geological processes vary greatly in rate and intensity—from slow and steady to sudden and "unusual" cataclysms. Thus they say that geological events are episodic rather than continuous.

Many violent geological processes are rhythmic because they are influenced by the motions of our planet. These motions produce the march of seasons and the consequent cycle of weather irregularities: droughts, floods, storms, avalanches, and tides. They can even trigger earthquakes and volcanic activity. Such events tend to be local, not of great moment in the history of the earth; however small changes accumulate over long periods of time and produce large results. Geological time runs slowly; viewed at that speed episodic changes tend to run together in an apparent continuum, much as the individual frames of a moving picture provide an illusion of smooth continuity.

Astronomic accidents, such as collisions of the earth with large meteors or even comets—dear to the hearts of some fiction writers—could, and probably have, produced worldwide geological results. Meteor impacts were not infrequent events in the early history of the solar system as the cratering of the moon and our neighboring planets indicates, but there is no direct evidence that earth-shaking collisions have occurred in the past several millions of years. On the average, rates of widespread geologic change are immensely slow by human standards.

The Legend of Noah's Flood

For scholars in the past, raised in the Judeo-Christian tradition, the greatest catastrophe of all was the Flood featured in the Bible's Book of Genesis. *"The same day were all the fountains of the great deep broken up, and the windows of heaven were opened, and the rain was upon the earth forty days and forty nights . . . and the mountains were covered"* (Gen. 7:11–22). Today's creationists still believe Noah's Flood to have been responsible for vast changes in the geological structure

Figure 4.2. Noah and his Ark. A woodcut dating from 1493. (Schadel's *Liber Chronicarum.*)

and surface topography of the earth, and this biblical story actually had an extraordinary influence on the early development of the science of geology.

The poetic story of Noah and his Ark is now regarded by thoughtful people as allegory. All of the modern zoos combined, with their thousands of trained keepers and elaborate facilities for feeding, housing, sanitation, and essential control of environment could briefly accommodate only a few hundred selected species of the millions that exist. As for plants—they were not even mentioned by the chroniclers of the Flood event.

The Flood story was not seriously questioned before the Renaissance. In the third century, Tertulian, second only to Saint Augustine in the formulation of Christian dogma, had expressed the view, reaffirmed and elaborated in 1282 by an Italian churchman, Ristoro d'Arezzo, that seashells, found frequently in the mountains, had been swept there by the catastrophe of the Great Flood. This explanation seemed reasonable enough until Leonardo da Vinci made a bold and accurate deduction, in 1509.

We like to think of Leonardo as an inspired painter, sculptor, anatomist, engineer, and inventor, but he was also a keen observer of geology. He superintended the construction of canals and selected stone for his sculptures in the great quarries of the Appenines. He thus had abundant opportunity to examine the fossil-rich rocks of Italy.

Rejecting the theological interpretation of fossils as relics of a universal deluge, Leonardo turned directly to nature for his explanations. He saw that the fossils were not simply strewn over the surface, but that the Appenines and the Alps were almost wholly composed of fossil-filled rocks. These had been exposed in high cliffs and valley walls that had been carved by rivers, long after being laid down beneath the sea. He deduced that the mountains were uplifted piles of river sediments and sea muds that had first hardened into shale, sandstone, and limestone, then folded and broken, and finally had been exposed to view by erosion.

Using his famous mirror-image script, he wrote in his notebook: "When the floods of the rivers, which were turbid with fine mud, deposited this upon the creatures which dwelt beneath the shallow sea near the shore, these creatures became embedded in this mud." Strata were formed, he surmised, not all at once or violently in a single catastrophe, such as Noah's Flood was said to be, but quietly, one at a time in sequence. They had none of the characteristics of torrential deposits. He noted that "in the mountain walls may be counted the winters of the years during which the sea multiplied the layers of sand and mud brought down by the neighboring rivers."

This remarkably modern interpretation of the significance of fossil sea shells unfortunately was not published until long after Leonardo's death. Indeed, the first book printed with movable type, the Gutenberg Bible, had only appeared some fifty years earlier, in 1454, and publishing was still in its infancy.

René Descartes' account of the origin of the universe appeared in the following century, and was an important effort to develop a scientific history of the earth; but his imaginative speculation was deficient in evidence, and unconsciously he borrowed much from Genesis. Five of his ideas were later taken up by fundamentalist "Flood" geologists:

First, the earth had a fiery origin; second, it evolved and changed through successive stages of cooling; until, third, a worldwide collapse of the crust occurred; followed by, fourth, a violent draining of a universal ocean into the earth's interior; and fifth, the draining torrents scoured the surface to produce present-day topography.

This idea of a physical origin of the world appealed to Thomas Burnet, an English clergyman who, in 1681, expanded the theory to feature Noah's Flood. Elements of Burnet can be recognized to this day in creationist writings on biblical catastrophism.

Burnet's *Sacred Theory of the Earth* took into account the fact that the volume of water needed for the universal ocean described in the Scriptures must have been much greater than the quantity now existing in the oceans. Indeed, it would have to be more than three times the known supply. So, he took the needed waters as rain from the atmosphere and then, after he had finished with the Flood, he disposed of the water into great caverns within the earth. We now know for certain from laboratory studies of the behavior of rocks under great pressures, and from geophysical soundings, that large caverns do not exist at great depths in the earth. Modern creationists therefore have to invoke an extra miracle to dispose of the surplus water of Noah's Flood.

Water is, indeed, contained underground, as shown by wells and springs, but the quantity, according to estimates by the United States Geological Survey, the official American government agency responsible for, among other things, information on hydrology, is only about 0.6 percent of all of the earth's water. If all the atmospheric moisture fell abruptly in a continuous worldwide rainfall, the level of the oceans would rise less than five centimeters; and if, at the same time, all the glaciers in the world melted (as they did many times in the past), sea level would rise only about sixty meters, barely enough to drown low coastal plains.

Geologists, with their new understanding of geological processes, had abandoned the Flood legend by the middle of the nineteenth century. Once they began to study sediments and their rock

Table 4.1 Water Necessary to Flood the Earth Completely

Present free water on earth	km^3
The oceans	1,322,000,000
Lakes and rivers	230,000
Glacial ice	29,200,000
Subsurface water	8,400,000
Atmospheric moisture	13,000
TOTAL	1,359,843,000

Water needed to raise the level of the ocean above present sea level	
Height in km	Water in km^3
1	402,900,000
2	889,900,000
3	1,389,900,000
4	1,894,300,000
5	2,402,300,000
6	2,911,800,000
7	3,421,800,000
8	3,931,800,000
9* (100% surface coverage)	4,441,800,000

* Height of Mount Everest: 8.8 km

equivalents they discovered that the rocks and fossils displayed the characteristics of many ancient environments besides the sea— e.g., lake, stream, marsh, and desert.

Flood theory then, as now, held that all sedimentary rocks had been violently deposited as sea mud and gravel, which were then exposed to the air, furrowed (while still soft), and eroded by unimaginably powerful currents as the sea suddenly left the lands. Present topography plainly contradicts these quaint ideas, for most of the vast plains and plateaus of the world are built not of sea muds but of river deposits, and they are totally incompatible with the concept of the existence of a universal ocean a few thousand years ago.

Great Floods of the Past

Several generations of geologists studying evidence along coasts and below the present sea surface have concluded that the sea was lowered during each of several Pleistocene ice ages. This resulted from the withdrawal of thousands of cubic kilometers of water to form glacial ice over the continents. Each ice age left the continental shelves dry for a time, but when the ice melted, the sea rose, advancing again over the shelves to rest at what are roughly the present shorelines.

Unhappily, recent research in this subject caught the eye of Fred Warshofsky, who published a sensationalized account under the title *Noah, the Flood, the Facts*, in the September 1977 issue of *Readers' Digest*. Warshofsky cited reputable scientific work as confirmation of Noah's universal Flood. He neglected to mention that this was not a new concept and that geologists had long recognized and mapped the successive levels in this last flooding of the continental shelves. Extensive flooding did, indeed, occur in earlier geologic periods, even long before man appeared on the scene, but at no time were the uplands covered.

The Great Spokane Flood in Idaho and Washington was a cataclysm, probably the greatest stream flood for which there is direct geological evidence. It occurred at the end of the last ice age when a melting ice dam released 3,300 cubic kilometers of

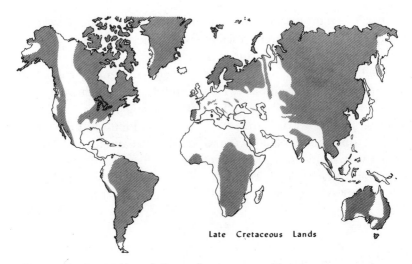

Late Cretaceous Lands

Figure 4.3. Composite of the total area covered by many repeated invasions of the sea over the continents in the Cretaceous period. Areas not flooded are shown by shaded pattern.

glacial lake water trapped in a tributary valley of the Columbia River. According to the U.S. Geological Survey, the water reached a maximum flow of about 64 cubic kilometers per hour, or approximately ten times the present flow of all the world's rivers. Old beach lines high on the hills above Missoula, Montana, show that the site before the flood was under 288 meters of dammed water. The volume of suddenly freed water rushed as an expanding wave over an area of nearly 8,000 square kilometers of plateau land spreading far beyond the confines of the original river valley. The result, as with smaller flash floods everywhere, was a peculiar braided topography unlike that of ordinary rivers. The topography thus produced is known locally as "channelled scabland."

Enormous ripples made of boulders and gravel were produced transverse to the direction of flow. The coarseness of deposits and the large scale of the pattern of erosion is a clue to the unusual violence of the event. While by no means a common event, the Spokane Flood is an example of perfectly natural, if cataclysmic, processes. If the flood geology of creationists were true, all the lands of the world would resemble the channeled scabland of Washington.

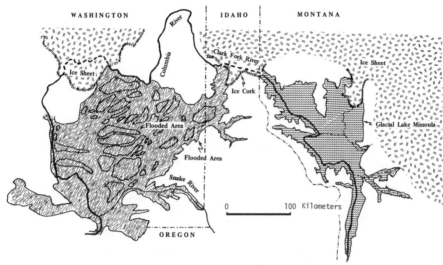

Figure 4.4. Great Spokane Flood at the end of the last ice age. (U.S. Geological Survey.)

Figure 4.5. Gigantic current "ripples" of boulders and gravel left by the Great Spokane Flood torrent. (Courtesy Dag Nummedal.)

Erosion of Landscapes

Normal erosion by rainwash and streams is most evident in areas of sparse vegetation and little soil. The Grand Canyon of Arizona and adjoining states is an awesome example of the power of a river system to erode the lands and carry away the debris. The canyon and its tributaries are frequently cited by creationists as evidence of Noah's Flood, yet it displays none of the characteristics of a cataclysm such as the Spokane Flood. While the canyon is exceptional for its great depth, the rock strata are not. In oil fields over the world the same general sequence of layered sedimentary rocks is encountered in deep borings. The particular interest in the Grand Canyon region and the high plateaus of southern Utah is that much of the total sequence of strata of the earth's crust can be examined here directly, without the need for deep drilling.

Viewed regionally, the plainly exposed sequence of fossiliferous strata in the Grand Canyon region forms a blanket several kilo-

Figure 4.6. Arizona's Grand Canyon southwestward from the North rim. An 1882 sketch by William Henry Holmes. (U.S. Geological Survey.)

Figure 4.7. Aerial view of Marble Canyon upstream from the Grand Canyon. Plateau surface is the result of slow stripping of soft strata from a limestone stratum. (U.S. Geological Survey.)

meters thick in which the fossils all belong to extinct species. Furthermore, each geologic division has its own species not found below or above. This is quite contrary to the hypothesis of the creationists, who argue that fossils are remains of organisms that all lived at the same time, together with members of present-day biota.

At the bottom of the Grand Canyon there is another sequence of much older (Precambrian) and less fossiliferous rocks that are tilted and overlain by the horizontal strata of the canyon walls. The lower series is a dramatic record of an earlier cycle of deposition, the tilting caused by earth movements, and deep erosion before the main canyon sequence was deposited.

Government surveys have shown that the Colorado River now carries each year enough mud and sand to lower the drainage basin an average of almost fifteen centimeters per thousand years.

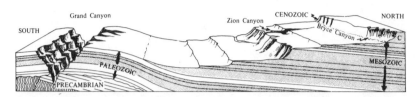

Figure 4.8. Sequence of rock strata in Grand Canyon region. Shaded strata are deposits of rivers, lakes, and desert dunes making most of the great thickness (7.5 km.) above the Precambrian. These rocks refute creationist contention that the sedimentary rocks here were deposited in Noah's legendary universal ocean. Length of section is about 160 km. (Redrawn from U.S. Geological Survey.)

This rate of erosion agrees with independent geologic evidence that the river system has been in existence at least 20 million years. There is simply no trace of a single, universal "catastrophe" here. Deposits of past seas in the region alternate with nonmarine deposits, several of which are ancient windblown dunes responsible

Figure 4.9. Wind-deposited dune of Jurassic age in Zion National Park, Utah. The eolian cross-bedding has been attributed by creationists to torrential deposition in Noah's Flood. (Edwin McKee, U.S. Geological Survey.)

for the spectacular scenery in Zion National Park and neighboring regions.

The Sedimentary Hourglass

Each layer of sedimentary rock anywhere in the world represents a depositional event among the fluctuating environments of sedimentation—river floods, storms, and other oscillations in supply and kinds of materials. The varied kinds and textures of rock strata show that conditions and rates of deposition were highly variable in the past, as they are at present.

The creationists would have the entire sedimentary blanket of the earth's crust deposited in the forty days and forty nights of rain of Noah's Flood. In their view there could be no conceivable source for the vast quantity of mainly fine-grained sediments. Close examination of the Grand Canyon rocks shows that, like sediments everywhere, they are composed of grains and fragments derived from preexisting rocks and soils of the land and from the skeletal parts of aquatic organisms. It takes long periods of time for the weathering of rocks to produce enough soil to form thick layers of sediment, or for millions of generations of marine animals and plants to live and die to produce accumulations of limestone tens or hundreds of meters thick. The hard shells of marine molluscs and brachiopods, and the skeletons of algae, sponges, and corals are today, as in the past, pulverized to fine sand and mud mostly by the activities of boring and feeding organisms, and their limy deposits display only the effects of slow and generally quiet deposition—no signs of "catastrophe" here.

While sedimentary rocks thousands of meters thick are common enough on the continents, the sediments in the deep oceans far from shore are almost invariably fine-grained in texture and usually only a few hundred meters thick. For millions of years the average rate of accumulation in deep waters has been only about one to five centimeters per millennium, as dated by geochronological methods. If flood geology were correct most of the sedimentary record would be in the deep oceans.

The rates of sea-floor deposition are even higher as we approach the continents, particularly at the mouths of rivers and estuaries, where as much as two hundred centimeters per thousand years accumulate. Even greater rates are observed within the continents. It is interesting that measured rates of sedimentation now taking place over the world are similar to those of the past.

A calculation of the average *maximum* rate of accumulation of the world's sequence of sedimentary strata on the continents has been made by Dr. J. D. Hudson of Leicester University in England. He selected the thickest, and therefore *on the average* the most complete, sequences of all the geological periods and plotted their thicknesses against their ages, as measured by radioactivity. He found an unexpectedly uniform *average* rate of rock accumulation of about thirty centimeters per thousand years, sustained for hundreds of millions of years. This general average is six to thirty times more rapid than deep sea sedimentation but does not, of course, take into account the many local variables. This work of Hudson's indicates long-term persistence of all the processes responsible for the stratigraphic column. It also rejects the thesis of creationists that the kilometers-thick sedimentary blanket was made at one time.

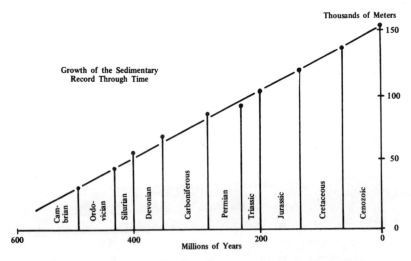

Figure 4.10. Average rate of accumulation of thickest rock units agrees with observed present-day rates. (Adapted from J. D. Hudson. *The Phanerozoic Time Scale.* Geological Society of London, 1964.)

Miraculous Catastrophism

Creationists would revive prescientific explanations and speculations about the origins of sedimentary rocks and fossils and the formation of mountains and canyons. Starting with the nonscientific premises of biblical Genesis, they invoke worldwide catastrophes because they consider the world young and they feel that slow changes could not produce the earth's features. Catastrophism is consequently axiomatic for the creationists. Even they realize that normal processes, including sporadic violent events such as earthquakes, work too slowly for the known results. Let the creationists demonstrate that normal processes at reasonable rates and frequencies are inadequate to shape the earth over vast spans of time. Surely, there is nothing blasphemous about regarding the Genesis story as nonhistorical. Science cannot disprove miracles, indeed it would be futile to try. The scientific way relies on known, testable processes.

5

Clues to the Past

> To produce a valuable observation, one has first to
> have an idea of what to observe. A preconception of
> what is possible. . . . The best world is the one that exists
> and has proven to work already for a long time. Science
> attempts to confront the possible with the actual. [François
> Jacob, *The Logic of Life*. New York: Pantheon Books,
> 1977.]

> *The physical processes which we can now study . . . can give*
> *us no clue whatever to the history of the Creation period; this*
> *latter history can only be known through divine revelation.*
> [Henry M. Morris, *Biblical Catastrophism and Geology*. Phil-
> adelphia: Presbyterian and Reformed Publishing Co.,
> 1974.]

The Dawn of Science

Historians like to point out that modern science, by extraordinary coincidence, started with the almost simultaneous appearance
of several monumental works, in 1543. Foremost was the epochal
De revolutionibus orbium coelestium by Copernicus, which ushered in
the scientific revolution. Another contribution, more directly influential in working out a history of life, was a profusely illustrated
folio on human anatomy, *De humanis corporis fabrica*, published by
Vesalius, a Belgian anatomy teacher at the University of Padua.
He demonstrated in detail that the human body, although undoubtedly inhabited by an immortal soul, was animal-like in every
physical feature.

The seventeenth and eighteenth centuries witnessed the beginning of the Age of Reason, a burst of scholarship by a dozen or
so European philosopher-scientists, among them Francis Bacon
and René Descartes, both of whom felt an affinity with nature
lacking among most earlier philosophers. Bacon, renouncing many

deeply entrenched theological prejudices, insisted that the only way to an understanding of nature lay in sound scientific observation. Most of the seventeenth-century scientists considered themselves devout Christians and accepted the Bible as man's spiritual guide, but not as a source of information about the natural world.

The First Cause

To Descartes and his followers, the "deists," it seemed reasonable for God to be seen through nature. God was the First Cause who created energy and matter in the beginning, leaving subsequent operation of the cosmos to His natural processes, the Secondary Causes. These men felt that if they were to learn about God, it would have to be through nature, not through intuition, revelation, or miracles. This has become the way of science and has been accepted by many enlightened religious people, who feel that the concept of an anthropomorphic God, embraced by most religions down through history, is an inadequate image for the Author of the universe—and no longer suitable for modern men.

In 1687, soon after the death of Descartes, Isaac Newton showed the world that the universe was not simply a fixed geometric pattern but, instead, a dependable "clockwork" machine consisting of mass, energy, gravity, and inertia. He stressed the idea that every natural effect has a natural (rather than supernatural) cause that could be studied and deduced from the results, even after a lapse of time. This principle has become an important aspect of both historical and experimental science. Newton brought about a marriage of the practicality of Bacon and the logic of Descartes. Newton argued that order in nature is mathematical order, that the past determines the present, and the present leads to and influences the future. Modern science, however, recognizes that history never repeats itself exactly. Every event is unique in some respect and chance deviations play an important role in nature.

Geological Laws

The work of the Danish physician, Steno, illustrates the idea of natural laws in historical geology. Steno left Copenhagen in 1660 to study medicine in Leiden and Paris where he achieved distinction as an anatomist. On arrival in Florence a few years later, he was appointed to a hospital post by Grand Duke Ferdinand II. There, apart from his regular duties as physician, he had time for field excursions and for research. He was later elected to the elite company of experimental scientists, the Accademia del Cimento, one of the forerunners of our academies of science.

During his excursions around Florence he discovered several principles basic for geologic history. Foremost among these was recognition that many geological features are the result of orderly development from demonstrable causes. Reasoning from evidence, he decided that the earth could not have been created in its present condition. His principles of stratigraphy, now known as Steno's laws, are considered essential to an understanding of the construction of the earth, and they form the mathematical basis by which geologists and engineers describe the manner in which water reservoirs are gradually silted, river plains built up, and strata formed.

The most important of these laws was the *law of super-position*, stating that layers of sediment accumulate sequentially, one at a time upward in chronological order. This principle establishes the relative age and position of every layer in a sequence of strata, much as a many-storied building is built from the bottom up; an analogy may be made to the pages of a history book. Another law, the *law of original horizontality* of sedimentary strata, is based on the observation that the silting of reservoirs and lakes, because of waves, currents, and gravity, tends to produce sediment bottoms that are flat and nearly horizontal; irregularities are covered and smoothed over by successive additions so that the depositional floor is leveled and nearly horizontal.

Steno recognized that in crumpled mountains, where the earth's crust has been uplifted and originally horizontal rock strata deformed, an understanding of the local complications depends on expert analysis of the geological conditions in adjoining undisturbed regions. Nowadays, these principles are regularly used in regional geological surveying.

The English scientist-philosopher, Robert Hooke, who was influenced by Steno's writings, studied and published in 1703

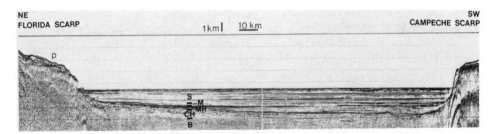

Figure 5.1. Cross-section of the Gulf of Mexico as recorded by a ship-borne seismic profiler. Section is about 240 km. long. Sea level shown above. The Gulf is a very deep basin about half-full of fine sediments thousands of meters thick similar to those now being quietly deposited by the Mississippi River. There is nothing to indicate violent deposition during the fourteen months of Noah's Flood as believed by creationists. (J. L. Worzel and C. A. Burke. "Margins of Gulf of Mexico." © *American Association of Petroleum Geologists Bulletin,* November 1978.)

descriptions and illustrations of fossil molluscs unlike those living today. Comparing them with the artifacts of ancient cities, he thought that the fossils might some day be useful in working out a prehistoric chronology of the earth far older than the history of mankind. Undoubtedly, Hooke's insight influenced later generations of British geologists who soon set out to develop a history of the earth.

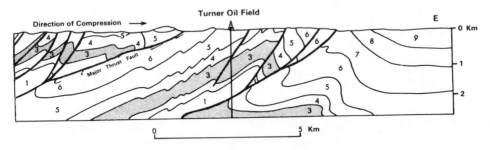

Figure 5.2. Overthrust belt near Calgary, Alberta. The underground relationships have been confirmed by intensive borings for oil. The depositional sequence of strata in individual blocks is not affected by the later deformation. Overthrusts do not invalidate the standard sequence of strata as claimed by creationists. (Redrawn and simplified from P. B. King. *The Evolution of North America.* Princton, N.J.: Princeton University Press, 1977.)

Creationism Reasserted

Philosophers of the next century, the eighteenth, trying to free themselves from the frustration and sterility of biblical revelation, speculated about an evolving universe; but a conservative reaction set in at the end of the century, just after the French Revolution, and religious orthodoxy was reasserted. Biblical creationism, firmly entrenched in Western thought for a millennium, was not to be so easily eradicated. With the reaction against the Age of Reason, widespread literal acceptance of the Mosaic story of Creation was restored, and almost until Darwin's contribution in the middle of the nineteenth century, scientists continued the task of defending church dogma, believing that if natural changes and geological ages were admitted, doctrine based on a strict reading of Genesis would be endangered.

The general level of knowledge of the earth in the eighteenth century is indicated in a thirty-four volume encyclopedia, *Histoire naturelle* by the popular philosopher-scientist, the comte de Buffon. The first three volumes of that important work appeared in France in 1748. It was sold out in six weeks and was translated in the same year into several foreign languages. It not only provided the public with the scientific knowledge then current, it also underscored late Renaissance scholars' efforts to break with medieval superstition.

Buffon was one of the first of the Western philosophers to grant antiquity to the universe. He gave the earth a minimum age of 74,000 years, or a more probable age of one million years, which he calculated from a laboratory experiment simulating the cooling of the earth from incandescence. His view of earth history was borrowed from Descartes but it went further, for he introduced the idea of organic evolution and geological epochs and he attempted to write a geological history. Theological authorities at the Sorbonne were outraged and Buffon was forced to recant publicly.

The Present is a Key to the Past

The long, slow climb toward a philosophy of earth history culminated in an epoch-defining publication, *The Theory of the*

Earth, published in 1788 by James Hutton. Educated as a chemist and physician, Hutton retired early as a gentleman farmer near Edinburgh and became a pioneer student of the origin and classification of soils and their conservation. In 1785 when he gave two lectures before the Royal Society of Edinburgh, he started a revolution in geology.

Isaac Newton had already stressed causality as a natural law and Hutton's friend, the Edinburgh philosopher David Hume, had developed it further: In all things cause and effect are related. That is, a given cause is followed by a characteristic effect. This is the essence of historical science. Hutton adapted it to geologic history—*a past natural cause can be deduced from its observed effects.* Eventually this came to be an axiom of geology: "the present is a key to the past"—working backward from the known present to the unknown past.

Hutton's special training made him realize that the mud, sand, and gravel of alluvial soils were mineral fragments derived from the disintegration of earlier rocks. Thus, if a rock stratum was composed of fragmental particles, it followed that the stratum represented a late stage in a history preceded by the formation and destruction of earlier rocks. From this basis and from observations of folded rocks of mountains, Hutton deduced a historical sequence, and demonstrated that the same sequence had been repeated several times in some regions: deposition of horizontal sedimentary strata derived from the erosion of older terrains, deformation of the strata to form mountains, deep erosion and wearing away of the mountains to form low hills, followed by renewed deposition and slow burial of the old mountain roots. His novel idea has since been confirmed in many mountain belts of the world. The Appalachians, the Rocky Mountains, and the Andes, for example, occupy the sites of much older mountains that were folded, uplifted, worn away, and then covered by new, flat-lying deposits from rivers and seas—a cycle that in some cases repeated itself over and over again.

These historical events, Hutton reasoned, proceeded in an orderly, cyclical sequence. He concluded that "an earlier world . . . is worn down while the waste products provide the materials for a new one . . . worlds without beginning, without vestige of an end."

The erosional discontinuity between folded mountain roots and an overlying blanket of flat sediments marks an interruption in the accumulation of a chronological sequence of rock strata known to geologists as an *unconformity*, or local gap, in the rock record of geologic history. The recognition of its significance was one of Hutton's most important discoveries. How many millions of years would be needed to wear down a mountain range to a flat plain not simply once, but many times, by the known agencies of weathering and erosion? Here was, indeed, substantial evidence of the vastness of geological time.

The Genesis story of Creation was so entrenched in the thinking of Europeans, however, that acceptance of Hutton's new geology would have been long delayed had it not been for the aid of his disciple and friend, John Playfair, professor of natural philosophy at the University of Edinburgh. Playfair, who had trained in mathematics and astronomy, thought that Hutton's theory resembled the successful method, already in use by astronomers, of calculating the immense orbits of comets from a few observations of their movements over a small arc and a short period of time; something of the vastness of the universe could be demonstrated with a small number of observations. In 1802, after Hutton's

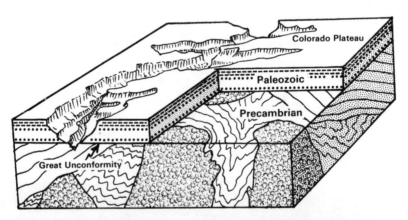

Figure 5.3. Unconformity in the Grand Canyon, Arizona. The disordered Precambrian rocks below were folded and intruded to form mountains. Then they were cut away by slow erosion to a low surface before the flat-lying strata were deposited. Hundreds of millions of years were required to complete the process.

death, Playfair published a popular account of the new philosophy entitled *Illustrations of the Huttonian Theory of the Earth*, sketching the outlines of Hutton's ideas on a broader scale and making them more understandable by means of familiar examples. The implication of the work of Hutton and Playfair was to eliminate miraculous causes as a serious explanation of geologic phenomena. They demonstrated to the satisfaction of many of their contemporaries that ordinary physical and chemical processes were adequate to explain the earth's structure and landscape. Hutton did not propose to eliminate God from the universe. On the contrary, he perceived a fabric, "erected in wisdom, to obtain a purpose worthy of the power that is apparent in the production of it . . . an order not unworthy of Divine Wisdom."

Lyell and Uniformity

Hutton and Playfair set the stage for Lyell's synthesis: the first systematic earth history. Lyell had become attracted to geology as a university student at Oxford, and by about 1825 he had concluded that the catastrophic events described in Genesis and still widely accepted in those days by both churchmen and geologists, were highly unlikely. He became a proponent of Hutton's working of natural laws and dedicated his life to expelling fantasies from geology. During the years 1830–1833 he published a treatise, the *Principles of Geology*, in three volumes, in which he brought together much evidence for an earth history based on reasoned inferences about past causes. It was an immediate success, going through twelve editions, and it formed an important link in the long chain of development of knowledge leading to Darwin's theory of evolution. Darwin later professed that Lyell had opened his eyes to geology and showed him how to think as a scientist. From Lyell, Darwin came to see nature as logical and orderly.

Using Hutton's logical method, Lyell made rational inferences about past events from clues preserved in the rocks. He interpreted these clues with the aid of mathematics, chemistry, physics, and biology—now the basic working method of historical geology. In his *Principles* he explained his philosophy: "My work . . . will endeavor to establish the *principle of reasoning* in the science . . . that *no causes whatever* have from the earliest time to which we can look back, to the present, ever acted, but those now acting." Thus, he undertook to eliminate unknown, contrived causes from geology. Geologists have adopted this methodology as eminently reasonable and successful, with the reservation, however, that allowance must be made for processes that were unknown in Lyell's day. He went on to say: the causes ". . . never acted with different degrees of energy from that which they now exert." Taken literally, most modern geologists would reject this statement as absurd, because even a casual examination of his writings shows that he admitted the occurrence of violent events such as meteorite impacts, sudden shifts in the earth's crust during earthquakes, floods, and volcanic eruptions. Clearly he was protesting the use of imagined agencies and not arguing that episodic processes were negligible in the shaping of the earth.

William Whewell, a contemporary of Lyell and a catastrophist, coined the absurd term *uniformitarianism* (now shortened to *uniformity*, perhaps as a joke, for what was really only the scientific principle of simplicity (commonly known as "Occam's razor"—it is idle to do with more what can be done with less)—if we review alternative explanations of phenomena, those should be favored that best fit the evidence. In other words, the hypothesis most likely to survive is the one that accounts for a maximum number of observations with a minimum number of assumptions. Uniformity is Hutton's rule that the present is a key to the past.

Creationists condemn this rule on the ground that only miracles can explain earth features because known processes operate too slowly and time has been too short.

Hans Kloosterman, editor of the journal *Catastrophist Geology*, at the Lyell Centenary Symposium, September 1975, in London, voiced a common prejudice against Lyell's uniformity: "Too many events in the earth's history do not fit a uniformitarian system— calderas, plateau basalts, ice ages, alpine nappes, bone breccias, the sudden appearance of diversified life at the close of the Precambrian, and the abrupt extinction of dinosaurs and ammonites, and so on."

These are favorite topics for creationists, who prefer miraculous to natural explanations. Yet, much of the science of geology is devoted to showing that these episodic phenomena are explainable by natural processes and by analogy with changes that can be observed to be taking place today. It seems to me tilting at windmills to argue that uniformitarianism must imply rigidly invariable rates of processes that always operate slowly. Few experienced geologists have been so deluded. Only creationists insist on characteristically violent and inexplicable processses in the history of the earth—this is what they mean by catastrophism.

Sampling the Past

Collecting evidence for excursions into the past is a sampling procedure. Observations on rocks and fossils constitute samples of real phenomena and provide many kinds of information. The reliability of the information depends on the problems under study, the kinds of answers being sought, and the sampling techniques. Alternative interpretations are assessed by the available means and conclusions must remain open to revision. Repeated cross-checking enhances reliability whenever the conclusions fit into a harmonious pattern with few discordant or unexplained items.

The evaluation of historical clues is not unlike a detective's reconstruction of a crime from circumstantial evidence, or like a trained tracking hound's identification of a scent while in pursuit of an invisible trail. In both cases past events are inferred from knowledge of cause and effect without the testimony (frequently unreliable!) of eyewitnesses.

Modern geology assumes that past earthly processes were not unique as viewed against the totality of geologic time and that past events and situations are best classified and understood in light of natural laws and materials.

Since past history cannot be directly observed, geologists study history-in-the-making both in the field and in the laboratory. This emphasis on observable processes is an application of a method used throughout all science of proceeding from the known into the unknown. Observations are made according to plan, and from the resulting data testable explanations are derived. This methodology differs profoundly from that of the creationists, who start with religious faith in miracles and then proceed to search for arguments that seem to support their presuppositions. Creationism is thus not science because those creationists who call themselves scientists are clearly placing their theology above their science.

Historical Science

Scientific research into the past is a search for historical "truth." The creationists like to say that all conclusions about the past are only "theories," a word that they use in the sense of unsupported speculation. Scientific theories about the past are based on verifiable "facts" (highly corroborated hypotheses) and they represent attempts to explain those facts.

What is scientific truth? Outside the laboratory, nature is so complex that observational information can always be counted as incomplete. But there is another, less evident difficulty. That is the perspective and experience of the investigator. Each person is likely to see what he or she thinks should occur. The strength of science is not that scientists are above error. Scientific knowledge is self-correcting through independent checks and counter-checks by many critical observers. In this respect historical geology and evolutionary biology are exactly like other branches of science.

During the 1979 celebration of Einstein's birth, there was surprisingly little notice given to Werner Heisenberg. Max Planck discovered the principle of quantum mechanics which Einstein criticized with his theory of relativity. Heisenberg was the famed German physicist who, together with the equally eminent Niels Bohr, elaborated Planck's theory of quantum mechanics which was difficult to reconcile with Einstein's theory of relativity but which provides an improved understanding of the structure of atoms. He derived from his study of atoms the "principle of uncertainty," an attitude that now pervades all branches of science.

According to Heisenberg the imprecision of knowledge is only partly because of deficiency in information-gathering. It is also a consequence of the limitations of the human mind and the nature of knowledge itself.

Physicists had generally adopted the deterministic view of the great early nineteenth-century French astronomer, Laplace, who argued that given enough knowledge of all the forces of nature and the positions of all objects of the universe, one could include in one formula their past and future movements in time and space—something like chess on a cosmic scale. In those days, physics and astronomy were considered "exact" sciences.

However, in 1927, Heisenberg demonstrated that changing configurations at the level of atoms have chance elements that cannot be predicted. Indeed, the simple fact of making an observation affects the result. It is impossible to determine simultaneously both the position and velocity of an atomic particle. The uncertainty principle and "complementarity" are the fruits of Heisenberg's unique perception of reality.

George Gaylord Simpson describes scientific truth in his *Concession to the Improbable* (1978):

A fact is something that can be observed and that can be confirmed by the observations of others. Worthy belief or, in some sense, truth, is interpretation of fact, and part of the scientific attitude is that any such interpretation is subject to correction. Truth in this sense can only be relative or tentative. This is hard for any of us to take, intolerable for children, young or old, who cannot tolerate uncertainty. One can, at least, be relatively certain that a belief contrary to the weight of factual evidence is not true.

Karl Popper, British philosopher, in his *The Logic of Scientific Discovery* (1968), has stressed that explanatory statements must be potentially capable of disproof (falsification) if they are erroneous. It is his view, and scientists agree, that corroboration is not enough to firmly establish a theory because favorable support may be unconsciously built into an explanation and because an endless number of positive observations will not rule out the possibility of significant negative observations.

Unqualified answers come slowly in science and there are degrees of falsifiability. Scientific problems often are complex and without clearly defined solutions. Even obvious answers usually involve some sacrifice of a familiar way of thinking or doing things in order to make progress to a higher level of understanding. The American philosopher William James once said that the appearance of one white crow can forever discredit the notion that *all* crows are black. But such a discovery would not advance understanding significantly. The existence of one albino crow among millions of black crows might be interesting, but it would not be statistically significant. The one piece of unexpected evidence is not enough to invalidate a general truth, namely that almost all crows are black. The scientist is more likely to be concerned with partial answers—frequencies, probabilities, and averages, than with the simple yes or no demanded by creationists.

Some explanations (theories), for example organic evolution by natural selection, are so all-embracing and involve so many branches of science and so much evidence, that they become supertheories, or paradigms, so sweeping in their implications that they cannot be subjected to simple tests of falsification. They must, therefore, be divided into subsidiary theories for either corroboration or falsification. Paradigms are not classifiable as true or false in their entirety but are valued for their usefulness in studying and understanding nature. Creationism does not qualify in this respect. It lacks evidence and explanatory content and it is in no way testable. Other than ostensible vindication of the Scriptures, what is its purpose?

6

Fossil Elephants Show the Way

> The history of life ceases to be hypothesis and inference and becomes direct knowledge when fossils are available. [G. G. Simpson and W. S. Beck, *Life*. New York: Harcourt, Brace & World, 1965.]

> *One should be wary of restorations of the past based on the fertile imaginations of paleontologists.* [John N. Moore and Harold S. Slusher, eds., *Biology: A Search for Order in Complexity*. A high school textbook of the Creation Research Society.]

Siberian Ivory

In the tenth and eleventh centuries, A.D., Arab traders developed caravan routes across Siberia into the Arctic from central Asia for a commerce in ivory. This commodity was in the form of great tusks similar in shape and quality to elephant tusks of Africa and India but often much larger. Elephants, however, do not live in Siberia.

The tusks were obtained by native "mammot" hunters who did not kill living animals for the ivory, but dug the tusks out of permafrost river mud and sand. Some historians think the biblical behemoth, pronounced "mehemot" by the Arabs, may have been derived from the native Yakut name for the Siberian mammoth.

Toward the end of the nineteenth century, the exportation of Siberian mammoth ivory had grown to some thousands of pounds per year. The route went through Yakutsk on the Lena River in eastern Siberia and was bound for Europe and southern Asia. Over hundreds of years of collecting, this could represent many thousands of individual mammoths, but such a figure does not take into account much larger numbers of unmarketable tusks and tuskless animals not reported by the hunters. The Chinese drew from the Siberian source of ivory as early as the fourth century B.C., and it is probable that much of the Chinese ivory for centuries had its origin in the graveyards of prehistoric Siberian animals.

N. K. Vereshchagin, leading mammoth authority at the Zoological Institute in Leningrad, has estimated that the one thousand kilometers of Arctic coastal plain between the Yana and Kolyma Rivers contain more than half a million tons of mammoth tusks with an average weight of thirty kilograms.

In the eighteenth century a native legend was still going around that underground monsters lived in the Siberian wilderness, but Europeans did not identify the mysterious beast until the French anatomist, Daubenton, demonstrated in 1762 that it was a kind of elephant. Toward the end of that century, three of Europe's leading zoologists—Cuvier, Camper, and Blumenbach—independently arrived at the conclusion that the Siberian fossil species, the "wooly mammoth," was unlike the two still-living elephants of the tropics, the African and Indian species, though somewhat more closely akin to the latter.

Cuvier and Extinction

The French scientist Cuvier is celebrated for elevating two branches of science, comparative anatomy and paleontology, above the purely descriptive level. Trained at the Academy of Stuttgart, he had his first professional appointment at the Museum d'Histoire Naturelle in Paris, as assistant to the professor of comparative anatomy. The following year, at the age of twenty-five, he gave a momentous public reading of his first paper comparing Siberian fossils and present-day tropical elephants. Because he was dealing with bones of enormous land animals that could hardly have been overlooked in the living fauna, he argued that the peculiarities of the fossil elephants must be taken as evidence that they were members of species that were no longer living. Previously, naturalists were uncertain whether living representatives of fossil species might turn up in some inadequately explored region. After all, they could cite biblical authority that all the forms that were needed were created, and that all persist today: *"I know that what*

God does lasts forever; to add to it or subtract from it is impossible" (Eccles. 3:14). After his success with the fossil elephants, Cuvier was excited by the prospect that many more of his fossils might be remains of extinct organisms and he devoted much of his life to discovering and describing them.

What Are Fossils?

The skeletons and tusks of the Siberian mammoths are fossils. The ivory, not petrified or distinguishable in most features from the Indian and African ivory, is nonetheless fossil ivory. Paleontologists learn about the past from fossils. According to dictionaries, the term "fossil" may be used informally for any outdated or old-fashioned thing, but paleontologists employ the word more precisely for skeletal remains or direct traces (such as footprints, impressions, burrows, etc.) of ancient animals and plants embedded in soil and rock layers. By general usage these must be older than the present historical epoch, at least 10,000 years, thus antedating the oldest written records.

Most fossils belong to species that are readily distinguishable by experts from any living organisms. That is, they are extinct. Fossil remains of still-living species are a relatively insignificant part of the fossil record limited to the shallowest, youngest, unconsolidated sediments. They represent only 1 percent or less of the history of life; the other 99 percent consist of kinds no longer living.

In summary, then, fossils are remains and traces of animals and plants of prehistoric age, nearly all extinct. The consolidated mud and sand in which they were originally buried hardened with the passage of time and increasing depth of sediment cover. Consequently, the older and more deeply buried examples are usually encased in rock and are brought to light only by deep erosion or by digging.

The History of Elephants

Fossils are always curiosities, but they have a much larger significance not apparent in a simple definition. They are the raw materials for learning about the ancient history of life, and they provide much information about the past that could not be obtained from other sources. Let me return to the dramatic example of the record of the elephants which, together with their near relatives, are called proboscidians; for they illustrate so well the historical significance of fossils.

Because of their large size and abundance in superficial river alluvium and swamp deposits over much of the earth, the bones and teeth of proboscidians were among the first fossils to attract attention. The ancient Greeks and Romans were known to have collected and exhibited them. The Siberian mammoth in the Old World, and the American mastodon in the New World were among the first fossil vertebrate animals to receive both scientific and widespread popular attention. It may accurately be said that the science of vertebrate paleontology started with the study of these majestic animals. The amazing extent of subsequent discoveries is indicated in a monumental work, entitled *Proboscidea*, published in 1942 in two great quarto volumes, by Henry Fairfield Osborn, one-time president of the American Museum of Natural History. Osborn recognized 352 species of proboscidians over the world of which 350 are known *only* from fossils. These figures are regarded as excessive by contemporary authorities, but the proboscidians were indeed diverse. The fossil examples are not duplicated by any variant forms among living elephants, but without the fossils we would know nothing of the history of the elephants.

The Woolly Mammoth

The most celebrated mammoth of all was discovered in 1899 along the Beresovka River, a tributary of the Kolyma on the Lena delta, some sixty miles north of the Arctic Circle. A Yakut ivory hunter came upon a nearly complete carcass of a mammoth with flesh and several organs preserved intact in the frozen ground. Very likely the hunter was already acquainted with other cadavers of this animal, because frozen mammoths still retaining bits of rotting flesh and hide had been reported since 1692 at a number of localities in northern Siberia. (In Alaska, they are encountered from time to time in river alluvium in the course of hydraulic gold mining.) Nevertheless, mammoths preserved in this way are extremely rare. The Beresovka specimen is now mounted and displayed in the Leningrad Zoological Museum, having been dissected and intensively studied.

In the summer of 1977, a gold prospector operating a bulldozer in frozen ground in northeastern Siberia on another tributary of the Kolyma, uncovered a complete six-month-old baby mammoth slightly over one meter long. This, the fifth and most complete

Figure 6.1. Baby mammoth in frozen river deposit, Siberia. This is only one of thousands of fossil mammoths along the shore of the Arctic Ocean. None of these occurs in marine deposits as required by the creationist idea that the animals were drowned in Noah's Flood. (Courtesy N. K. Vereshchagin.)

mammoth carcass with skin and organs preserved by freezing, is now on display in Leningrad beside the Beresovka mammoth. The field evidence and radiocarbon analysis indicate that the baby mammoth, who was named Dima, was buried in a bog or small lake by a mudslide about 44,000 years ago.

The adult woolly mammoth was approximately as tall as a modern Indian elephant, with similarly infolded grinding teeth but it differed in several important respects. It had a conspicuous bony topknot containing large sinuses and had only four skeletal toes instead of five. Its body was covered with long, coarse black hair and thick underfur, and beneath the skin was a layer of fat up to eight centimeters thick. The tusks were relatively longer, heavier, and somewhat more curved than those of modern elephants, and the back sloped downward more steeply from the shoulders to the hindquarters.

A cold to cool climate is clearly indicated for the woolly mammoth by the heavy coat of hair and the layer of insulating fat, and the common occurrence of its remains near glacial deposits in association with the fossils of other Arctic animals, such as the hair-covered woolly rhinoceros, musk oxen, reindeer, and a distinctive community of many now-extinct animals. According to Russian botanists, the stomach contents of several frozen examples of the woolly mammoth have yielded some eighty species of well-known northern grasses, sedges, and trees of high-boreal and tundra areas. Migrant mammoths certainly made their way long distances south of the continental glaciers in both Eurasia and North America, much as the present African elephant roams for great distances.

We are accustomed to thinking of elephants as tropical animals, but viewed over their long history they evidently have been at home in a great variety of climates. Zoologists have concluded from studies of African elephants (described by Peter G. Hiley in *Natural History* magazine, December 1975) that they are not especially equipped physiologically for life in a hot climate.

In spite of the apparent freshness of some of the mammoth remains, there is no evidence that these, or any of the many other extinct elephantlike species, survived into the postglacial epoch. Several species of mammoths thrived throughout much of the northern hemisphere and Africa during the second half of the Pleistocene ice age. Then they became extinct just as the last of the great ice sheets were melting away. Glaciation was not the cause of their extinction; however, a climatic change and man's activities may have contributed to it. The coincidence in time is much too striking to be ignored.

Many radiocarbon dates of woolly mammoths from Siberia, the Ukraine, Europe, and North America indicate that the mammoth disappeared throughout its immense range about 10,000 years ago, about 8000 B.C., the youngest average date that keeps recurring with impressive frequency. From the evidence it would appear that mammoths did not survive for long even in isolated places after that date.

Mammoth Extinction Legends

The general causes of this dramatic episode of extinction are conjectural, and specific causes may never be known with certainty. However, there is no evidence that the extinctions were caused by a worldwide cataclysm such as Noah's Flood, a belief widely held by eighteenth- and nineteenth-century scientists and still favored by creationists. The fossil skeletons are never found in marine deposits, although isolated teeth have been dredged from the continental shelf, which in any case was dry land several times during the ice age.

Frozen mammoths figure prominently in discredited hypotheses of catastrophic extinction. The glacial geologist William R. Farrand made a careful survey of present knowledge and opinion among mammoth experts and reported his findings in a 1961 issue of *Science* magazine (vol. 133, p. 729), where he concluded that gradual climatic changes may have eliminated the Siberian mammoths.

Other Relatives of the Elephant

The woolly mammoth was only one of many different wide-ranging members of elephantlike animals living in a variety of climates over the world. Twenty-seven species of mammoths have been named in North America alone. The order Proboscidea consists of two great groups which, according to E. H. Colbert, the vertebrate paleontologist, are "as different as cats from dogs." One of these groups, the mammoths and living elephants, is divided into eight or ten large branches, or *genera*, each subdivided into many species. The other group, the mastodons, is much larger and is wholly extinct. Osborn divided it into thirty-one genera and many more species.

Mammoths have only two, high-crowned, grinding teeth below and two above, and these have many simple, transverse ridges of enamel that wear down into plates by use. Tusks are lacking in the lower jaws. The mastodons were in many ways more primitive. They had a lower, more massive body, several low-crowned cheek teeth, and commonly a pair of lower as well as upper tusks. The geologically oldest mammoths show traits transitional with mastodons, which suggest that an even earlier mastodon was their common ancestor.

The American Mastodon

Like the mammoths, the mastodons were exceptionally tolerant of varied climatic conditions, and produced many local races all the way from Alaska to Patagonia. At least one northern species was woolly. The mastodons first appear in the fossil record in Egypt, well before the oldest mammoths. Later they spread gradually out of Africa, where the record is most complete, into Eurasia and North America, and finally into South America. The place of origin and direction of migration are inferred from the first appearances in the various regions where they have been found.

The mastodon attracted the fascinated attention of pioneer Americans and still makes headlines in many parts of the United States. Over six hundred mastodon sites are on record for the northeastern United States alone. Since many of the discoveries are in peat bogs, where these animals frequently became mired, bogs are considered favorable sites for hunting mastodon skele-

Figure 6.2. Probable area of origin and subsequent spread of the evolving elephant family as indicated by distribution of fossils. Shaded areas indicate present range.

tons. During the past decade, for example, two discoveries have been made in bogs in New Jersey within a few miles of my home. Nearby Orange County, New York, is a veritable mastodon graveyard with many swamps in which the remains of hundreds of these animals have been found.

One of the most interesting and historically important of these was collected under the direction of Charles Willson Peale in 1801 and restored and mounted for exhibition in Peale's famous Philadelphia Museum, first in the hall of the American Philosophical Society, and later in the building now known as Independence Hall. George Gaylord Simpson, writing in 1954, noted that it was the first essentially complete mastodon discovered, the first fossil skeleton of any kind to be mounted in America, and among the first in the world. It was part of a collection purchased by P. T. Barnum in 1850 and was later sent to Germany, to be housed in a museum in Darmstadt. Another specimen was found in 1925 by workmen at a building site on Dyckman Street west of Broadway at the northern end of Manhattan Island. Part of this was salvaged, and is now at the American Museum of Natural History.

Public attention was first directed to these animals in 1706 when the governor of Massachusetts received a strange gift that two Dutch colonists had found in a Hudson River bank, south of Albany. It consisted of gigantic leg and rib bones and a huge molar tooth weighing several pounds. The governor and a friend, the Reverend Cotton Mather, agreed that the relics most probably belonged to a prehistoric man, one of those "accursed giants" mentioned in Scripture as having been destroyed in the rising waters of the Great Deluge of Noah.

At about the same time, settlers in western Pennsylvania were hearing from Indians about monstrous bones at Big Bone Lick, a salt marsh in Kentucky about twenty miles southwest of the present city of Cincinnati. The lick was said to contain great skeletons with ivory tusks several yards long and heads pointing to a common center. Specimens were eventually brought to President Thomas Jefferson in the White House and later sent to London and Paris where they were identified as a kind of elephant. From the fresh appearance of the bones, Jefferson was convinced that the mastodon must still be living somewhere in the unexplored wilderness of western America. Parts of scores of mastodons have since been removed from Big Bone Lick together with bones of many other extinct mammals of the late Pleistocene age. Most probably they were trapped in soft mud while seeking salt.

Knowledge gained by more than two centuries of research on mastodons in the Americas and elsewhere indicates that they flourished in many regions as contemporaries, both of mammoths and of early man, until and end of the Pleistocene ice age when they and many other large land animals abruptly disappeared. Radiocarbon measurements indicate an average age of about 10,000 years for the youngest specimens now known, but many

Figure 6.3. The mastodon was prey for early humans. (Mural at University Museum, Madison, Wisconsin. Painted by Gregg Klees and reproduced here by permission of the *Milwaukee Journal*.)

specimens give dates older than this. Like the mammoths, they disappeared in a wave of extinction of large mammals.

The Evolution of the Proboscideans

Proboscidea first appear as smallish piglike animals that are closer in appearance to tapirs than to modern elephants. As we search backward in time the genealogical trail grows dim, not because of lack of suitable candidates for ancestry, but because the earlier groups do not closely resemble living elephants. The great heyday of the Proboscidea came very late in the history of life. Their remains are found in shallow, unconsolidated stream and swamp deposits at the top of the youngest part of the fossil record.

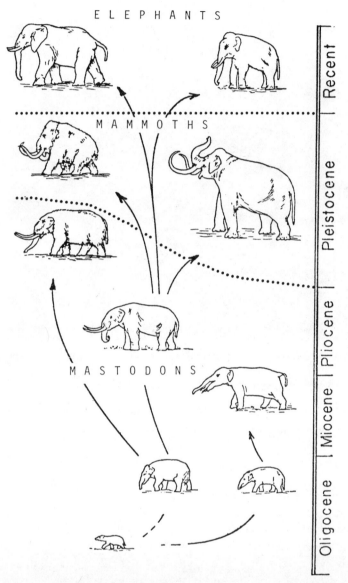

Figure 6.4. A greatly simplified history of the elephants and their relatives based on fossils. (After H. F. Osborn. In C. O. Dunbar. *Historical Geology*. New York: John Wiley, 1933, fig. 306.)

This distribution renders false the old idea that all animals were created more or less simultaneously and therefore that they should be distributed more or less evenly throughout all the thousands of meters of fossiliferous strata. They are not.

Fossil Elephants Illustrate Historical Principles

While interesting in itself, the story of fossil elephants and their near relatives can be used to illustrate the various kinds of information that can be gleaned from fossils. Scientific work in paleontology, as in other fields of science, may be classed in four stages: exploration, description and comparison, evaluation and testing of hypotheses, and development of mature theories. Paleontology is concerned not only with accumulation of facts about fossils, but also with the formulation of integrated conclusions about their historical significance.

It is worthwhile now to review the kinds of evidence that paleontologists use to reconstruct a history of the past.

1. Since fossils generally can be identified and classified by detailed comparisons with other fossils and with living animals and plants, they are recognized as records of past life.
2. Fossils occur, scattered or concentrated, where they were buried within layer on layer of sedimentary strata, or hardened beds of sand and mud. The fossils are uncovered either by erosion or by excavations that sometimes reach thousands of feet beneath the surface.
3. Together with the enclosing rocks, the fossils reflect varied environmental conditions, often unlike those existing today at the site. For example, alternating layers of the undisturbed debris of fresh-water swamp vegetation and sea shells frequently occur in rock strata of high mountains; palm leaves and crocodile bones are found at many places in the rocks of Arctic regions.
4. Most fossils belong to species and genera that are now extinct. Only the youngest and most shallowly buried examples are identical with, or most like, kinds now living.
5. In the total stratigraphic sequence of fossils a few were long-lived. Mostly, however, each kind is restricted to a limited

part of the sequence and generally does not reappear at lower and higher levels. No species ranges throughout the whole sequence of strata. The sequence of kinds of fossils is similar at closely spaced localities. At more widely spaced places deviations become pronounced, but general resemblances are still apparent and permit recognition of a world sequence of faunas and floras.

Each of these aspects of the fossil record suggests historical development, and taken together they provide the basis for a complex history of the earth and its life: profound changes of climate, hundreds of instances of flooding of large portions of the continents by shallow seas, repeated upheaval of mountain ranges, and the successive changes in organisms, as we trace similar kinds through the rock layers of the earth's crust. It is clear that organisms and their environments have undergone great and persistent changes.

7

Treasures from the Past

> The paleontologist is interested in how organisms leave a record in sediments, potential future rocks. . . . But the record may also be a trace of its activities and thus of the behavior of a living animal. [Wilhelm Schäfer, *Aktuo-Paläontologie*. Senckenberg Research Institute, Frankfurt-am-Main, Germany, 1962.]

> *Fossils . . . clearly give evidence of rapid burial and therefore catastrophism. They support the catastrophist model more directly and obviously than the uniformitarian model.* [Henry M. Morris, ed., *Scientific Creationism.*]

The Origin of Fossils

If you enjoy a stroll in the woods and fields, try asking yourself where are the remains of the great hosts of plants and animals that have lived and died there. Countless generations of organisms have come and then disappeared without recognizable traces. If you glance about, you will see an overwhelming preponderance of life, and very little evidence of death. True, the vegetation at temperate latitudes seems to die back each year in the fall; leaves wither and drop, grass turns brown. But the roots of perennials live on year after year and even the annuals continue by means of their seeds and spores. Animals are usually less conspicuous than plants, but small kinds are diverse and abundant in the sheltering vegetation, where they find both lodging and board.

How can fossils be formed from these organisms? With a little reflection we arrive at the correct answer. For the most part, the dead bodies of plants and animals are quickly eaten or are decomposed by bacteria and fungi. Because plant and animal tissues contain much water, when they dry out they wither.

Oxidation also aids bacteria in this process of decomposition. Organic matter is thus recycled as food by the living generation. Were this not so, the soil would quickly become sterile and organic litter would pile up to such depths that new plants would be smothered and the animals would starve. Even bones and shells will disintegrate within a few years if they are exposed to the air. To become fossils they must escape destructive processes by being covered quickly and thereafter protected from corrosive waters. Quick burial, however, does not require a catastrophic event. Normal sedimentary processes suffice.

The factors affecting the scattering of shells and bones before burial and their preservation after burial have been systematically studied by paleontologists using present-day examples and environments as guides. For the most part, bones of land animals are not found in marine deposits even though they might be floated or swept into the sea during stream floods. Characteristically, they are concentrated in deposits of river flood-plains and channels in association with fresh-water mussels, fossil wood, and leaves. Clay strata interbedded with the bones frequently show polygonal mudcracks and raindrop prints formed by exposure of the sediment in intervals between floods. The condition of logs and bones usually indicates very little, if any, transportation and abrasion, or disturbance by scavengers. By analogy with present conditions it is likely that occasional concentrations of whole skeletons represent animals that were mired in the mud and quicksand of shrinking waterholes where they were buried by flash floods. Some rare examples of skeletons in various death attitudes suggest animals smothered and buried by sandstorms or by the ash of volcanic eruptions. (See figure 7.3.)

Leaves, insects, and small animals drop into the quiet waters of lakes and marshes and sink to the bottom, and if the bottom waters are poorly aerated, the organic remains are less disturbed by scavenging worms and bacteria. The bodies of small terrestrial and flying creatures become buried whole and occasionally join the fossil record with the fine microscopic details preserved.

Inevitably, aquatic organisms are preserved in much greater abundance than others because their life environments in lakes and seas are favorable for quick burial in poorly oxygenated

Figure 7.1. Dinosaur bones in hardened river alluvium. The scattering is a result of predator activity and stream action before burial. The animal was not drowned in a marine flood. (Dinosaur National Monument, Utah. Courtesy Rebecca Lawton.)

Figure 7.2. Fossil amphibian of Permian age taken from the rock slab shown in *A*. (Courtesy W. Swinton, British Museum.)

Figure 7.3. Rhinoceros of Miocene age buried by volcanic ash in northeastern Nebraska. (Courtesy Michael Voorhees, Nebraska State Museum.)

sediments. The oxygen content of the sediments drops with increased concentration of organic matter so that fossils are likely to be more abundant and better preserved in fine-grained sedimentary rocks rich in organic matter. Well-aerated bottoms usually support a rich fauna of burrowing worms and other scavengers that churn the sediments to depths of many centimeters in search of food.

It is interesting to note that the processes of burial leave a highly selective fossil record. Because of the lack or presence of hard skeletons or shells, some groups are readily preserved, others are not. Organisms that live at sites of sediment accumulation are favorably situated for preservation, others are not. Even the subaqueous sediments of a richly inhabited lake or sea may be so much disturbed after deposition that the resulting fossil record is poor or lacking. As a sample of a once-living biota, any fossil assemblage is always incomplete or, as paleontologists say, strongly biased.

Kinds of Preservation

Many types of skeletal parts, for example, bone, wood, clam shells, are filled with organic matter during life. After death, much of this disappears and the pores, when filled with minerals, are then much heavier and more solid than the original. This type of fossil is said to be petrified, although the term is rarely used by professional paleontologists. In other cases, the skeletal remains are preserved with hardly any mineralogical change.

One of the most remarkable examples of the preservation of organic tissues in antiseptic swamp waters is a nonmarine "fossil graveyard" in Eocene lignite deposits 45 million years old in the Geisel Valley of East Germany. Extinct animals, including groups rarely found as fossils—monkeys, snakes, and birds—were trapped in small, scattered bogs where they accumulated and were preserved in stagnant waters. Many thousand remains of vertebrates and a larger number of insects, molluscs, and plants were found in these deposits. Many of the compressed remains of soft tissues show details of cellular structure, and some of the specimens had undergone but little chemical modification. Among the frogs were specimens in which the bones were leached away while the brain and spinal cord were preserved. Muscle tissue, connective tissue showing microscopic detail and cartilage were found in fishes, frogs, salamanders, lizards, and mammals. Small details of fly larvae and beetles, including muscle tissue and tracheae, were preserved.

Several fossils contained remains of fat cells and pigment cells.

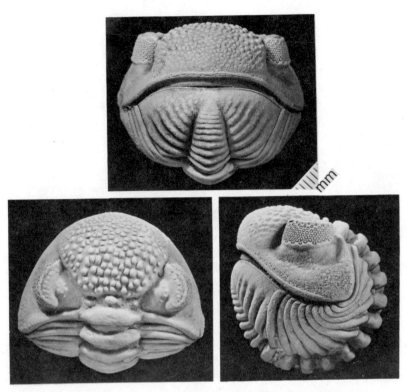

Figure 7.4. Devonian trilobite from the Spanish Sahara. Enlarged about X1½. (Courtesy Niles Eldredge, American Museum of Natural History.)

Well-preserved bits of hair, feathers, and scales probably are among the oldest known examples of essentially unmodified preservation of such structures. The stomach contents of beetles, amphibia, fishes, birds, and mammals provide direct evidence about eating habits. Bacteria of two kinds were found in the excrement of crocodiles and others were found on the trachea of a beetle. Fungi were identified on leaves, and the original plant pigments, chlorophyll and coproporphyrin, were said to be preserved in some of the leaves. From such ample fossil evidence, the Eocene terrestrial life of the Geisel Valley has been reconstructed in considerable detail.

A fairly common and very important preservative of invertebrate fossils and plants is silica, the main constituent of ordinary glass. Fossils preserved with this flinty substance are sparingly scattered throughout the stratigraphic column. They are hard and chemically exceedingly resistant, and so frequently are the best preserved elements in fossil assemblages. A familiar example is petrified wood composed mainly of silica in the form of opal, chalcedony, chert, or quartz. In the best preserved examples the silica impregnates the cellulose soon after burial under conditions that inhibit bacterial and fungal decomposition. The finest and most delicate cellular details are preserved this way for hundreds of millions of years. Siliceous impregnation may be regarded as a kind of embalming under antiseptic conditions in a moisture-proof, airproof matrix of extremely fine-textured minerals.

In another mode of silicification, there is no impregnation of the original skeletal material which, in fact, has been dissolved away by seeping ground water and replaced by silica. Microscopic fabrics of the original material usually are not preserved, and the fossil is only a replica—in some cases a very perfect replica—

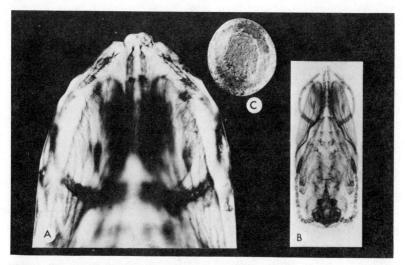

Figure 7.5. *A, B:* Silicified fossil insect larva (a midge) greatly enlarged; from Miocene lake deposit, southern California. *C:* Limestone nodule, X⅔, similar to that which contained the insect. (Palmer, U.S. Geological Survey.)

Figure 7.6. Brachiopods of Permian age from Pakistan. Originally the shells were calcareous until they became fossilized by resistant silica. The matrix was dissolved with acid, permitting the exposure of exquisite details. Approximately natural size. (Courtesy Richard Grant, U.S. National Museum.)

of the original surfaces of the shell or skeleton. These silicified fossils may be extracted from the hard rock matrix by means of appropriate acids. As an illustration of the importance of this kind of preservation, G. Arthur Cooper at the National Museum of Natural History in Washington, D.C. extracted an estimated 5 million invertebrate fossils from approximately sixty tons of selected blocks of 250 million-year-old (Permian) limestone collected in Texas.

A major obstacle in the study of fossil vertebrates has been the tedious and difficult mechanical extraction of bones from hard rock matrix by grinding and chipping. The principal constituent of bone is calcium phosphate which, unlike limestone, is relatively insoluble under natural conditions, and which must be freed chemically or by manual cleaning under a microscope with small tools.

Abundance of Fossils

Strata considered to be only sparsely fossiliferous when judged from superficial inspection may actually contain an abundance of fossils. The degree to which this is true is shown clearly by methods of bulk collecting, wherein a volume of sediment or rock is gathered and the nonfossil matrix later removed in the laboratory. Bulk collecting has long been used for microscopic fossils such as plant spores and foraminifera, but it is also used effectively for the bones and teeth of small vertebrates and shells of brachiopods and molluscs. The number of fossils thus obtained can represent a far greater number than can be collected at the surface. Furthermore, fossils collected in matrix are commonly of better quality than those that have long been exposed to corrosion and disintegration. The limiting factor, one of the great deterrents to effective paleontology, is that only under certain conditions can the matrix be easily removed.

In many strata small fossils are incredibly numerous and are

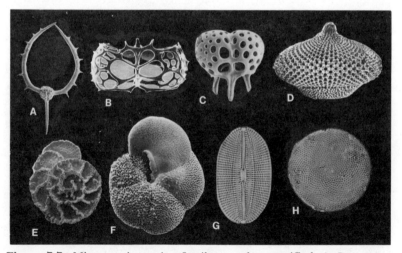

Figure 7.7. Microscopic marine fossils, greatly magnified. *A–D:* Radiolaria. (Courtesy Robert Goll.) *E–F:* Foraminifera (Courtesy Exxon Production Research Co.) *G–H:* Diatoms (G. W. Andrews. "Diatoms." *Micropaleontology*, vol. 26, no. 15, 1980.)

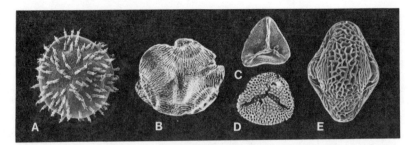

Figure 7.8. Spores and pollen of land plants, greatly magnified. Such fossils are most abundant in nonmarine strata. *A:* Lower Carboniferous spore, Australia. (Courtesy Geoffrey Playford.) *B—D:* Permian spores, Australia. (Courtesy E. Kemp.) *E:* Late Cretaceous–Tertiary. (All published in *Journal of Australian Geology and Geophysics,* Vol. 2, no. 3, 1977. Reproduced here by permission of the Director, Bureau of Mineral Resources.)

major components of the rocks. Joseph Leidy, a leading nine-teenth-century American anatomist and paleontologist, once estimated a quarter of a million foraminifera in an ounce of marine sediment. Coccolithophorids, which make up part of the phytoplankton of the ocean, are one-celled flagellated algae with an armor of beautiful calcareous plates, the coccoliths. These plates are now accumulating on the sea floor as a vast blanket of fine

Figure 7.9. Coccolithophores, marine phytoplankton. The tiny disks of calcium carbonate are so small that one cc. could contain billions of the plates. (Courtesy Andrew McIntyre, Lamont-Doherty Geological Observatory.)

Figure 7.10. Chalk cliffs at Dover, England. Part of a widely distributed quiet-water marine deposit composed mainly of coccoliths. At the present time similar deposits accumulate at less than one to only a few mm. in a thousand years.

white paste, the main constituent of chalk. The individual plates are so small that a cubic centimeter of pure coccolith ooze contains thousands of millions of coccoliths.

Robert Broom, a South African paleontologist, estimated that there are 800,000,000,000 skeletons of vertebrate animals in the Karroo formation. While this guess may be reasonable, nevertheless we can confidently assume that only a few hundred good skeletons will be accessible at the surface and eventually discovered and removed by competent collectors. Any estimates, of course, are only suggestive, but they stress the vast difference between the collected sample and the astronomic numbers of fossils remaining buried. The discovery of a fossil species plainly depends on the intensity of the search and the numbers of fossils that are accessible at, or near, the surface.

Steady improvement in techniques of collecting and extracting fossils has effected a revolution in paleontology in the past few years, and has shown that there is a bountiful supply of material available for the stout of heart equipped with technical knowledge and suitable equipment. The great impediment to progress in paleontology is not so much the limitation of the record as the small number of experts in the field, and the difficulties inherent in freeing fossils from matrix in preparation for study.

The fossil record is rich only in selectively preserved skeletons and traces of organisms that lived mainly in low places or in water. It is deficient in many kinds of plants and animals, especially soft-

Figure 7.11. Collecting fossils for fun and science in an Upper Carboniferous formation along Mazon Creek, Illinois. Here amateurs collaborate with scientists of Chicago's Field Museum. (Courtesy Gordon Baird, Field Museum of Natural History.)

Figure 7.12. Fossil spider of Upper Carboniferous (Pennsylvanian) age, Mazon Creek, Illinois. (Courtesy Gordon Baird, Field Museum of Natural History, Chicago.)

bodied forms and those that inhabited well-drained uplands or other places exposed to weathering and erosion. In spite of these limitations, some sedimentary rocks contain excellently preserved soft-bodied organisms, and these tell us much about past life and environments.

Fossil collecting for scientific study has become a sophisticated art. The invasion of this field by commercial collectors and marginal amateurs often results in an insensitive vandalism to the most accessible fossil sites. Both state and federal agencies are belatedly trying to impose long overdue restrictions on fossil collecting, but such restrictions tend to be unenforceable. There is as yet unrealized potential for cooperation between serious amateurs and professional paleontologists to join their efforts in a systematic exploration for records of past life, especially in the proliferation of man-made excavations that provide ever new access to fossiliferous rocks.

8

The Fossil Calendar

The relative time of existence of a vast number of kinds of animals and plants has now been established, and their place in the geologic column has been confirmed by the co-operation of geologists the world over. This is not a theory derived *a priori*, but a discovery painfully and tediously worked out by the systematic study of the faunas of rock formations carefully located in the geologic column. [Carl O. Dunbar, paleontologist, in *Historical Geology*. New York: Wiley, 1949.]

Modern speculation has managed to distort the testimony of this sedimentary graveyard into a fictional record of slow evolutionary development over a billion years of imaginary earth history. This strange notion has indeed today become accepted and taught as scientific fact in most of our educational institutions all around the world. [Henry M. Morris in John C. Whitcomb, Jr., *The World that Perished.*]

The Sequence of Fossils in Geological Time

One of the truly great scientific discoveries of all time, essential to an understanding of the history of the earth, was made by an unsophisticated English civil engineer unacquainted with evolution. His name was William Smith. His discovery forever discredited the old fantasy that the sedimentary rocks of the outer part of the earth's crust and their fossil record of past life were all deposited together within a few month's time in the great Flood of Noah, as related in the Bible. Furthermore, he laid the groundwork for a geological time scale, ultimately the basis for the evolutionary history of life, not vice versa.

In the eighteenth century advances in mining and civil engineering created a demand for a system of comparison and classification of the rock sequences of scattered districts. It was an early practice to apply local names to noteworthy rock units, or "formations," as they were called.

Inevitably the more enterprising mining men would seek to clarify their problems by comparing and contrasting different mining districts, and such comparisons led to questions concerning conditions responsible for the mineral deposits. But the method of dating and correlating these events in geologic time had to wait for Smith's discovery. Formation units had been distinguished by their physical characteristics, but many separate units were similar in appearance. Smith then demonstrated that the fossils at successive levels in the rock sequence showed unique, nonrepeating characteristics by which rock layers could be positively identified and arranged in the chronological order in which they were laid down in ancient bodies of water.

The Earth Acquires a History

By the end of the eighteenth century the Industrial Revolution had brought prosperity to Britain and had stimulated many advances in science and technology. Both the theoretical and practical aspects of science are usually interwoven and this relationship between basic science and industry is well illustrated by rapid advances at that time in stratigraphy and paleontology.

It was becoming self-evident to the naturalists that the earth had a geologic past, and that nearly all the fossil record preceded the advent of man, the human record forming only the latest short chapter in earth history. The idea of changes in the history of life was soon followed by the discovery of the sequential introduction from time to time of increasingly complex groups of organisms from lower to higher strata. The invertebrates, some of them quite complex animals, long preceded the vertebrates in the geologic record. Fish preceded land animals and plants, and reptiles appeared before mammals and birds. Recognition of these facts was followed by increasing consideration of the possibility of organic evolution.

These facts of observation were in conflict with the views of the

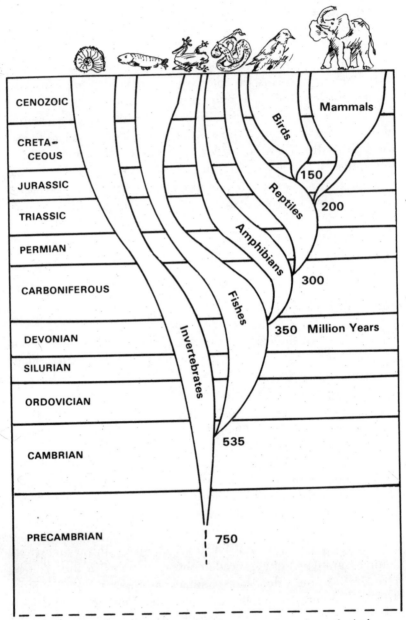

Figure 8.1. Major groups of vertebrates appear in a chronological sequence that agrees with their order of complexity. This is contrary to the creationist expectation that they were all created together at the base of the fossil record.

biblical creationists who, thinking that the earth's surface topography must date from the Great Flood, claimed that the "more active and intelligent" species, when confronted by the peril of the rising flood waters, tried to escape by assembling on high places before they were drowned and preserved as fossils in the flood muds.

Even today the creationists have officially adopted this quaint fantasy in their 1974 guide to public school teachers, *Scientific Creationism*, edited by Henry Morris. In this they say "the general order from simple to complex in the fossil record . . . considered by evolutionists to be the main proof of evolution, is thus likewise predicted by creationism only with more precision and detail."

International exchange of information on regional stratigraphy soon made it clear that sequences of fossil animals and plants are quite independent of present altitude and topography. In fact, the geologically youngest strata with the most advanced fossils usually are found in low places such as river basins. Well-known

Figure 8.2. Canada's highest peak, Mt. Robson, is composed of very old (Cambrian) fossiliferous marine rocks slowly lifted high above sea level while they were deeply carved by rivers. (By permission, National Film Board of Canada.)

assemblages of both land and sea organisms that are discovered at depths in mines and canyons in one area occur elsewhere in the same relative sequence in high mountains; the enclosing strata evidently had been depressed in one area and uplifted in the other. It is the place in the sequence that matters, not the elevation.

William Smith's Contribution

Between 1791 and 1799, William Smith, with the help of a clergyman, the Reverend Benjamin Richardson, developed a new method of geologic surveying. At the age of eighteen, Smith was a land surveyor's assistant, and in subsequent years he traveled about England and Wales observing rock outcrops and noting the kinds of soil formed by the weathering of different kinds of rocks. He studied borings for coal and water and did underground surveying in mines, gradually becoming fascinated by the fossils he found throughout the English countryside.

In response to demands for coal by booming industries, the British Parliament appropriated funds for the Somerset Coal Canal, and Smith was commissioned to survey the best route for it. In the course of his work he noted that many of the rock layers, or "beds," changed in thickness and character from place to place, but he found that the fossil assemblages maintained their general characteristics and lay in the same relative sequence throughout the region of his study. In spite of gradual changes in rock characteristics from place to place, he could keep track of the sequence and depths of strata by reference to the fossils.

Smith was soon identifying all the principal formations and accurately predicting the nature and depths of buried strata from the data that he had compiled, and he found that fossils permitted him to match outcrops and correlate sequences many miles apart. The conclusions thus arrived at were tested by drilling and by observations in mines and other excavations. Eventually he could accurately predict thicknesses and other details of underground rock layers from observations at the surface. Thus, the depth to coal seams and other commercial rocks could be accurately predicted before beginning operations. This method of prediction before drilling is now routine in geological exploration.

Smith had virtually no knowledge of biology, so at first he could neither classify nor name his fossil shells, and his work was purely descriptive. He was, however, extremely methodical and his work contributed substantially to the development of natural resources and the improvement of roads and waterways.

Smith was not a scholar, and there is no evidence that he was influenced by the field studies and opinions of continental geologists. He was born in 1769, the same year as the great French paleontologist Cuvier, but the two had little else in common. Smith's modest means and lack of leisure prevented him from publishing his geological map of England and Wales, based on fossil content, until 1815, by which time his methods of mapping formations according to their geologic ages had been widely publicized and tested by geologists throughout Europe. A few years after his map appeared William Smith, with the help of Richardson, published a table of the characteristic fossils of each formation. This drew wide attention to the possibility of placing the fossiliferous layers in an international stratigraphic framework.

The Sequence of Fossils

The international geologic time scale that eventually emerged was a product of stratigraphic studies by practical men who had neither knowledge of, nor interest in, organic evolution. It is important to note that some of the basic principles, and a broad outline of the standard international stratigraphic system now in use by geologists, were established and widely used by 1840, nearly two decades before the publication of Darwin's theory of evolution. The thousands of meters of fossiliferous rocks that form the outer part of the earth's crust have acquired meaning through evolutionary theory, but the fossil sequence, although it illustrates evolution, was not established to aid the argument for evolution, nor does evolution depend on the fossil sequence. Rather, the two reinforce each other.

Zonation

Distinct assemblages of species and genera, usually designated by the Latin name of one of the organisms, are called biostratigraphic zones. These follow one another in a nonrepetitive sequence marking off identifiable stratigraphic intervals, thus providing the key for dating and correlating events over the world in standard "ages," "epochs," and "periods."

Figure 8.3 illustrates how the world sequence of graptolites, an extinct group of marine invertebrates, serves to establish equivalent stratigraphic sequences in widely separate regions.

The sequence usually is not complete at any one place because not all strata are fossiliferous and sedimentation has not been continuous, even in the ocean basins. Creationists view the fact of local incompleteness as evidence which discredits the concept of a world system of stratigraphy. But let us imagine hundreds of copies of a book each of which has random gaps where pages or entire chapters are missing. Comparison of all the copies can easily provide material for a complete text and for the exact placement of yet undiscovered fragments of the same book.

The Geologic Time Scale

Fossils provide a basis for world stratigraphy and a relative time scale for dating long past events by means of assemblages of fossils in common. Creationists frequently charge paleontologists with circular reasoning: Fossils are assigned to a geologic period—say, the Cretaceous—if they are found in Cretaceous rocks, *and* rocks are dated as Cretaceous if they contain Cretaceous fossils. This is a distortion of the facts, for it is the position in the whole *sequence* of fossils that determines the relative age of an assemblage of fossils and rocks. Each successive fauna and flora follows predecessors in a predictable order based on experience and each in turn gives way to younger and higher assemblages in a relay that is only intelligible as a product of evolution.

The term "geologic system" was early applied to major biostra-

	Zones	Great Britain	Eastern North America	Australia	USSR
DEVONIAN	*Monograptus yukonensis*				X
	M. falcarius				X
	M. hercynicus				X
	M. praehercynicus	Zones absent in Great Britain, but present in Thuringia, D. D. R.; Yukon, Canada Bohemia; and Podolia and Middle Asia, U. S. S. R.		X	X
	M. uniformis		X	X	X
	M. angustidens				
	Pristiograptus transgrediens				X
	Monograptus perneri				
	M. bouceki		X		
	Saetograptus lochkovensis				
	Pristiograptus ultimus				
	P. fecundus				
	Saetograptus linearis				
SILURIAN	*S. leintwardiensis*	X	X	X	X
	Pristiograptus tumescens	X	X	X	X
	Cucullograptus scanicus	X	X	X	X
	Neodiversograptus nilssoni	X	X	X	X
	Pristiograptus ludensis	X	X	X	X
	Cyrtograptus lundgreni	X	X		X
	C. ellesae	X			X
	C. linnarssoni	X			X
	C. rigidus	X		X	X
	Monograptus riccartonensis	X	X	X	X
	Cyrtograptus murchisoni	X		X	X
	C. centrifugus	X			X
	Monoclimacis crenulata	X		X	X
	M. griestoniensis	X	X	X	X
	Monograptus crispus	X	X	X	X
	M. turriculatus	X	X	X	X
	Rastrites maximus	X	X	X	X
	Monograptus sedgwicki	X	X	X	X
	M. convolutus	X	X	X	X
	M. gregarius	X	X	X	X
	M. cyphus	X	X	X	X
	Cystograptus vesiculosus	X	?	X	X
	"Akidograptus" acuminatus	X		X	X
	Glyptograptus persculptus	X	X	X	X
ORDOVICIAN	*Dicellograptus anceps*	X	X		X
	D. complanatus	X	X	X	X
	Pleurograptus linearis	X	X	X	X
	Dicranograptus clingani	X	X	X	X
	Diplograptus multidens	X	X	X	X
	Nemagraptus gracilis	X	X	X	X
	Glyptograptus teretiusculus	X	?	?	?
	Didymograptus murchisoni	X	X	X	X
	D. bifidus	X	X	X	X
	D. hirundo	X	X	X	X
	Isograptus caduceus	X	X	X	X
	Didymograptus nitidus	X	X	X	X
	D. deflexus	X	X	X	X
	Tetragraptus approximatus		X	X	X
	Clonograptus tenellus	X	X	X	X
	Dictyonema flabelliforme	X	X	X	X

Figure 8.3. The sequences of graptolite species and genera are closely matching in widely separated regions. They illustrate the basis for a worldwide calendar of geological time. (Courtesy John Riva.)

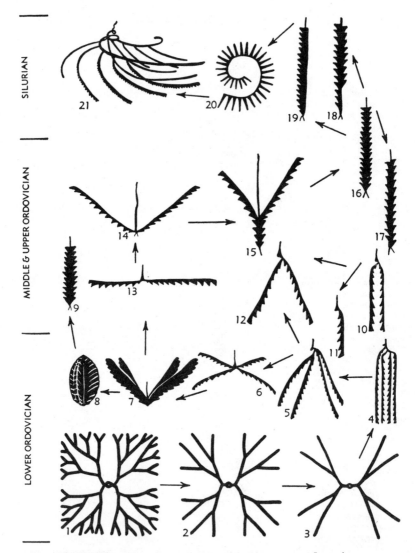

Figure 8.4. Graptolites, an extinct worldwide group of marine invertebrates whose evolution has provided many chronological zones. Arrows show directions of evolution in a few of the many families. (From Moore, Lalicker, and Fischer. *Invertebrate Fossils.* © 1952. Used with the permission of McGraw-Hill Book Company.)

1790	1840		Modern			
Post-Diluvial Diluvial	Alluvium	Cainozoic	Holocene Pleistocene	Quaternary	Cenozoic	Phanerozoic
Tertiary	Pliocene Miocene Eocene	Cainozoic	Pliocene Miocene Oligocene Eocene Paleocene	Tertiary	Cenozoic	Phanerozoic
Secondary	Cretaceous Jurassic Triassic	Mesozoic	Cretaceous Jurassic Triassic		Mesozoic	Phanerozoic
Transition	Permian Carboniferous Devonian Silurian Primordial	Palaeozoic	Permian Carboniferous Devonian Silurian Ordovician Cambrian		Paleozoic	Phanerozoic
Primary	Primary	Azoic	Ediacaran (or Vendian)		Precambrian	

Figure 8.5. Evolution of the fossil calendar.

tigraphic divisions recognizable over much of the earth. Each had its own unique assemblage of fossils and was named for a region (e.g., Jurassic, Jura Mountains) or for some characteristic feature (e.g., Cretaceous, chalk; and Triassic, threefold). By about 1840, a widely accepted table of named systems had come into general use. Each system was regarded as the rock record of a period of geological time. They have since been continuously refined and subjected to tests of usefulness and validity by the world's geologists, who have diverse needs and interests.

About 1840 John Phillips, a nephew and apprentice of William Smith, proposed a grouping of the geologic systems into even larger divisions or eras—Paleozoic, Mesozoic, and Cainozoic (Cenozoic)—recognizable by the prevalence of particular orders and classes of animals and plants but exhibiting clearly and unequivocally transitions from one system of life to another. He chose natural boundaries corresponding to what he took to be episodes of extinction and sharp dwindling in the world's biotas.

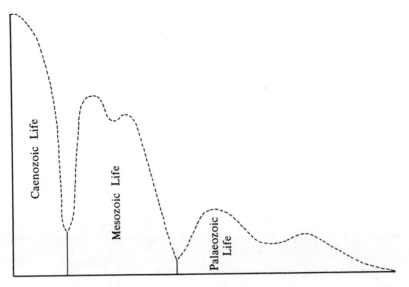

Figure 8.6. The geological eras were based on biological "revolutions" at the beginning and close of the Mesozoic. (Phillips, 1860.)

The Lyell and Deshayes Contribution

Important contributions to the development of the geological time scale were made by Charles Lyell when his *Principles of Geology* appeared in 1830. In subsequent years he focused attention on the need for developing a uniform classification of the geologic sequence, the central pillar of earth history. More than anyone else, Lyell synthesized the evidence that led to a universal system. His personal influence with the world's leading geologists and the success of his book made the geological time scale essentially a British invention.

Lyell brought to England great collections of fossils from Sicily, northern Italy, and France gathered from rock sequences called Tertiary. This Tertiary System derived its name from the fact that it was the upper thick blanket of extremely fossiliferous, frequently soft sediments and rocks overlying more compact Secondary (Mesozoic) rocks containing strikingly different fossils. The "basement complex" of apparently unfossiliferous mainly igneous and metamorphic rocks comprised the Primary System.

The Parisian biologist, Paul Gerard Deshayes, Europe's leading authority on molluscs, studied Teritary fossils with Lyell in the late 1820s and early 1830s. Their general conclusion was a statistical demonstration of the time-significance of fossils, and the Tertiary became the youngest geological period in Lyell's classification. Primary and Secondary were later to be replaced by other terms.

Lyell and Deshayes documented the sequential characters of the Tertiary molluscan assemblages and showed that there was a simple mathematical relationship between stratigraphic position of the fossil assemblages and their resemblance to still-living marine forms. The stratigraphically higher assemblages most closely resembled present-day marine faunas. The two investigators devised a novel scheme of subdividing and correlating the Tertiary "by reference to the comparative proportions of living species of shells found in each." Although modified and refined by later work, their general conclusion that the living fauna appeared gradually in the latter part of the Cenozoic era has passed all tests.

Basing the divisions on percentages of still-living species of molluscs, Lyell formulated five rock series, equivalent to geological time "epochs" (see table 8.1).

A few years later, paleontologists carved a sixth epoch, the Oligocene, from the Upper Eocene and Lower Miocene, and a seventh, the Paleocene, was separated from the Lower Eocene. This work with Tertiary molluscs is important because it was the first rigorous test of the chronological order of fossils, and it was an independent corroboration of the gradual replacement of older forms by the modern fauna. Modern, more sophisticated work amply confirms the evolutionary nature of the fossil succession and the Lyellian method of dating rocks.

D'Orbigny's Stages

It was the Frenchman, Alcide d'Orbigny, who showed how to subdivide the older geological systems of pre-Tertiary rocks in which there are no still-living species and relatively few surviving genera and families. D'Orbigny, an expert with marine invertebrates, was an outstanding field naturalist who traveled widely and knew the international literature of paleontology as well as anyone. He divided all the systems, including the Tertiary, into subordinate units of strata, "stages," that bear closely similar fossil assemblages over the world. The value of the d'Orbigny stage was soon demonstrated and has subsequently proved to be very useful for paleontological correlation and dating when tempered by the fact that fossil faunas usually succeed each other less abruptly than he thought. Many new stages, further subdivided into zones, have

Table 8.1 Lyellian Method of Dating Rocks

Epochs	Still-living Molluscan species
Recent (Holocene)	100%
Pleistocene	90
Pliocene	33–50
Miocene	18
Eocene	3.5

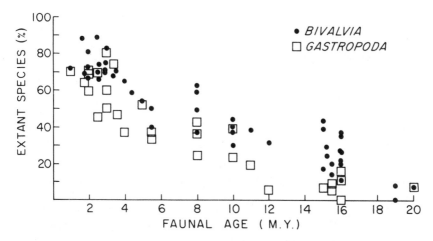

Figure 8.7. History of tropical Pacific mollusks. The points represent assemblages of species from various localities in America and Japan. The graph is a modern corroboration of Lyell's method of dating strata by percentages of modern forms found as fossils at successive stratigraphic levels. (Steven M. Stanley, et al. From "Lyellian Curves in Paleontology." *Geology*, a publication of the Geological Society of America, September 1980.)

been added to his original list, permitting refined international comparisons by age equivalence.

Pre-Darwinian Paleontology

The steadily increasing need for reliable information about fossils early in the nineteenth century led to the publication of ponderous descriptive catalogs in Europe and America mainly by English, French, and German scientists. These books provide us now with a fair overall view of the status of paleontology in pre-Darwin years.

An outstanding example of a university textbook that appeared in the 1840s was by François Jules Pictet. This and other general works show that a consensus had already been reached on salient characteristics of the fossil record without the explanatory benefits of evolution theory. These conclusions, arrived at empirically, are

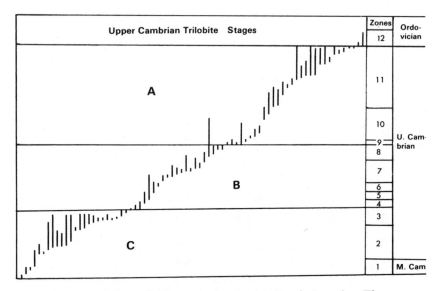

Figure 8.8. Cambrian trilobite zones in western North America. These illustrate d'Orbigny's *stages* and the way in which fossil ranges (vertical bars) tend to overlap. (Simplified from Slitt, Oklahoma Geological Survey.)

still valid today:

1. Assemblages of distinctive species characterize major stratigraphic units and the geologic time divisions which they represent. There is a piecemeal, sequential replacement of old by new assemblages. Once a particular fossil assemblage as a whole drops out of a sequence it does not reappear as such, although some conservative elements may long survive.
2. Differences between fossil and comparable living assemblages increase with geologic age.
3. Marine assemblages are frequently sandwiched between assemblages of land plants and animals, coal beds, old soils, and other evidence of land conditions. This much-repeated observation indicates hundreds of advances of the sea over the land, alternating episodes of deposition in seas, fresh waters, and marshes.

These characteristics of the stratigraphic record made known by Smith, Cuvier, and others were confirmed by later generations of practical geologists, many of whom were persuaded by the evidence of their own observations that biblical geology could not explain the plain facts of the fossil record. The groundwork for a geological time scale based on fossils was completed before geologists started to think about a history of life.

World Mapping of Fossiliferous Rocks

Today, geologic mapping based on the age-classification of fossiliferous rocks is far advanced worldwide, both on land and on the sea floor, and stratigraphic sequences have been divided and subdivided in detail. In addition to the international units, thousands of local minor units have been named and incorporated into regional maps. In the United States alone, millions of water wells and over 2 million borings for gas and oil averaging many kilometers deep, confirm and establish beyond question the reliability of the stratigraphic framework and the sequence of fossils established so long ago.

The floor of the sea is being systematically drilled and the sequences of fossils studied by a cooperative international Deep Sea Drilling Project (JOIDES). Countless continuous echo-soundings by ship-borne geophysical instruments are also contributing to our knowledge of stratigraphy.

The measurement of time requires irreversible change. Time, like the flight of an arrow, is unidirectional. Smith's discovery of

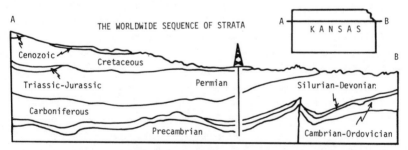

Figure 8.9. Rock strata underneath the state of Kansas penetrated and confirmed by thousands of deep wells. The evidence tells of scores (not simply one, as required by the creationist "model") of marine floods that alternated with times of land emergence and deposition of river alluvium. (Adapted from Kansas State Geological Survey.)

the uniqueness of each successive fossil assemblage supplied such a measure. The time-dependence of the sequence of stratigraphic subdivisions, combined with Lyell's concept of geological history, provides a key to understanding the origins and distributions of many useful mineral deposits and fuels in the earth. Hence, the fossil calendar is constantly put to the test and improved by successive generations of practical geologists, most of whom, even today, are not concerned with explanations about organic evolution. Yet the fossil calendar and its stratigraphic system are perhaps the very best single test of evolution. They refute the old thesis of simultaneous creation of all life at the beginning of the geological record.

Early in the twentieth century, physicists discovered a method of translating the biostratigraphic divisions into ages measured in years. Finally, a geological time scale became available measured in uniform units rather than the relative units of the fossil calendar. This will be the subject of the next chapter.

9

The Geological Clock

It has not been found possible to alter the rate of disintegration of any [radioactive] product by any external agency. [Lord Rutherford, *Radioactive Transformation.* Cavendish Laboratory, Cambridge, England, 1906.]

The highly speculative nature of geochronology seems rather obvious in the light of the many assumptions involved. . . . When one considers the dogmatic way its questionable findings are used, he is appalled if not indignant at the apparent intellectual dishonesty involved. . . . It appears that geochronology is an example of a mixture of assumptions, guesses, and imposed imagined universal principles. [Harold S. Slusher, *Critique of Radiometric Dating.*]

Theological Time

Early Christian scholars as far back as Saint Augustine in the fourth century thought the universe was about 6,000 years old, a figure obtained by adding up biblical genealogies. Shakespeare was well acquainted with this date, which he mentioned in his *As You Like It,* written in 1599. The Anglican Archbishop Ussher was responsible, in 1654, for dating Creation at 4004 B.C.; this date appears in the margin of many Bibles, where it was inserted long ago by an unknown editor.

A few years later (1658), Vice-Chancellor John Lightfoot of Cambridge, one of the greatest Hebrew scholars of his day, confirmed Ussher's date and calculated further that God had created Adam out of the dust of the earth on Friday morning, September 17, 4004 B.C. at nine o'clock. These romantic ideas, conceived in the childhood of Western civilization, have now generally been put aside. (*"When I was a child, I thought as a child;*

but when I became a man, I put away childish things"—1 Cor. 13:11.)
Modern creationists have pushed back the date of Creation to
about 10,000 years ago, a date that contrasts markedly with the
4.6 billion years for the earth and more than 15 billion years for
the universe considered reasonable by geologists, cosmologists,
and astronomers. The creationists cannot accept such early dates,
for to do so would seem to destroy the basic assumption of their
theory.

Absolute Time

"How old is that fossil?" And, "how do we know?" These are
questions often asked of geologists, and the answer is usually given
in relative units of the fossil scale. But years (as determined by
radiometric methods) are increasingly used because they provide
a uniform scale for measuring rates of change. Geochronology
involves a composite interplay of many independent lines of
evidence. Such criteria as sequence, kinds of fossils, oxygen
isotopes, radioactivity, and terrestrial magnetism are checked
against each other for agreement (*concordance*). Geochronological
ages are given in years B.P. (before the present).

Some Properties of Atoms

One of the most important achievements of physics is a general
understanding of the properties and behavior of atoms. All
physical phenomena originate in the two properties of atoms—
mass and force. The latter includes nuclear forces that bind
together the components of the atomic nucleus, and the electro-
static attraction between the orbiting electrons and atomic nuclei.

In spite of their chaotic, random, and unpredictable motions,
electrons are as dependable as anything we know. When an
electron makes a transition from one energy state to another it
assumes a frequency proportional to the energy change. These
differences are fixed by atomic laws and are invariable for each
chemical element. For example, the element *cesium* used in atomic

clocks vibrates at 9,192 megacycles per second. This, in effect, is the ticking of the cesium clock. It should be stressed that the frequency rate is not theoretical; it is known from actual measurements.

Atomic Clocks

For thousands of years men kept records and measured time by two motions of the earth, the rate of rotation and the length of the trip around the sun. These motions are slightly erratic; consequently, until recently the most accurate clocks required continuous adjustments—insertions of leap years and even leap seconds—to agree with a twenty-four hour day and a year of 365 days. Radio time signals from Greenwich, England, have long provided coordination for the world's clocks.

However, since January 1, 1972, a different method has been adopted throughout the world—atomic time in clocks which run at a constant rate independent of the length of the day. Radio time signals are now based on atomic time, an international system known as universal coordinated time (UTC), with an accuracy around 10^{-12} (i.e., one trillionth of a second). Such precision is not needed for the ordinary affairs of humanity, but it is important for pinpointing geographic details on earth by satellite, for high-speed navigation, and space exploration. An early example of the advantage of extreme precision in time measurement is provided by spaceship Mariner 10, which was off course only 60 kilometers near Venus after having traveled 150 million kilometers. Even greater accuracy is now possible.

The accuracy of ordinary quartz timepieces and the control of radio and television oscillators that accurately fix wavelengths is also dependent on the atoms that make up molecules of crystalline quartz.

Radioactivity

Geologic dating in thousands or millions of years is also based on the properties of certain radioactive atoms. The story of radioactivity and the atomic age began in 1896 when the French physicist, Antoine Henri Becquerel, showed that uranium compounds spontaneously produce invisible rays. Ernest Rutherford, the English scientist, later found that such radiation is of three kinds: alpha rays (nuclei of helium atoms), beta rays (electrons), and gamma rays (electromagnetic radiation similar to x-rays but of higher frequency).

The decay of radioactive substances conforms to a law described in 1902 by Rutherford and Soddy. None of these can exist indefinitely and the time necessary for any initial number of atoms to be reduced to one half is called its halflife. For radium, the halflife is short, 1,622 years; for the element plutonium (a common poisonous waste from nuclear power plants), the halflife is 24,000 years.

Since the early days of nuclear science there has been a general understanding that the rate of emission of alpha and beta rays, the emissions employed in dating geologic events by a radioactive substance, is independent of external changes in environment. Acceptance of this conclusion is based on thousands of laboratory experiments over the world. Precise modern measurements have suggested that exceptional conditions in the laboratory can induce small rate variations ranging from 0.1 percent to 3.5 percent in certain elements, but this is under conditions not likely to exist naturally and these particular substances are not used in age dating.

Radiometric Dating of Rocks

Bertram B. Boltwood, a physicist at Yale University, was the first to obtain radiometric ages of rocks. He suggested in 1905 that the ultimate product of the radioactive breakdown of uranium was lead, since it is invariably present in all uranium minerals. From the chemical analyses of forty-three uranium samples from localities over the world he showed that geologically older samples contained more lead than the younger ones, and that those of the same fossil age had the same uranium–lead ratio.

In this work, Boltwood computed the ages of ten mineral

samples ranging from 410 million years for a Connecticut uran-
inite, to 2,200 million years for a specimen of the same mineral
from Ceylon. These ages were so much greater than previous
estimates based on other criteria that few geologists were then
willing to accept them. However, the uranium–lead method of
determining absolute ages has steadily grown in credibility and
now is regarded as highly reliable within the ranges of sampling
and laboratory errors.

The Age of the Earth

Creationists, without giving their evidence, think that the earth
is 10,000 years old. Geologists believe it to be more than 460,000
times that old. Arthur Holmes, English pioneer in geophysics, made
an interesting observation that bears on the theoretical age of the
planet. Three isotopes of lead commonly occur together in deposits of
this metal throughout the world. Two of these, lead 206 and 207, are
derived from the disintegration of two forms of uranium with
different halflives. Consequently, these forms of lead start to accumulate as soon as the parent uranium crystallizes from solutions.

The third isotope, lead 204, is not the product of radioactivity,
so it does not change in abundance with time. Holmes argued that
growth curves of the ratios of lead 206 and 207, plotted against
the invariant 204, projected back through time, should provide a
date when only lead 204 was in existence. After many analyses,
Holmes obtained a hypothetical age of 4.5 billion years, which he
thought should provide a minimum age of the earth.

Subsequent work by many investigators has refined this estimate
to somewhat more than 4.6 billion years. Two additional age
sources seem to confirm this theoretical calculation. A class of
meteorites thought to date from the birth of our solar system
consistently gives an isotopic age of about 4.6 billion years, a date
also obtained from the oldest moon rocks. Consequently, geologists, cosmologists, and astronomers take this date as the most
likely time of origin of the earth and the other planets of our solar
system. Earth rocks of this age have not been discovered; the

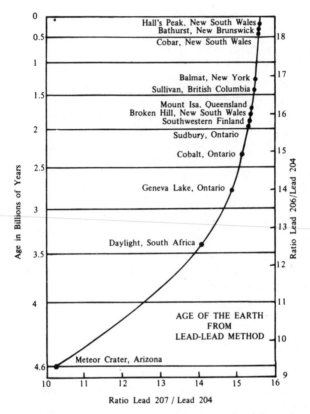

Figure 9.1. The age of the earth determined from isotopes of lead. Three kinds of lead occur together in nature. Two of the three are daughter products of uranium isotopes; the third is nonradiogenic and does not change in quantity, thus serving as a standard for evaluating the changing ratios of the other two. (Stephen Moorbath. "The Oldest Rocks in the Growth of Continents." © *Scientific American*, March 1977. All rights reserved.)

oldest rocks known at the time of this writing are metamorphosed sediments about 3.8 billion years old, in West Greenland.

The perfection of extremely delicate procedures of analysis now provides several independent radiometric methods for dating rocks based on isotopes of uranium 238 and 235, thorium, rubidium, potassium, carbon, and others.

Concordance—Cross Verification

Radiometric dates are tested by cross-checking by independent laboratories, with different samples, and by checking them against the results obtained from more than one isotope pair. To be acceptable, a date must conform with other dating methods such as geologic sequence and fossil zones. The objective is neither to defend an hypothesis about evolution nor to demonstrate the antiquity of the earth, but rather to learn the age of some geological event.

Numerous pairs of analyses based on different series of isotopes at separate laboratories have been made on moon rocks. In a summary of this work, the Canadian geochemist L. R. Armstrong has reported that rubidium/strontium and argon 40/argon 39 dates from each sample were highly concordant, differing by only about one percent and ranging between 3 and 4 billion years for different samples.

Radiocarbon

In many ways the most interesting and by far the most versatile radioactive isotope is carbon 14, which has made extraordinary contributions to studies of ocean currents, the history of the sea floor, past climates, and archaeology, and has been used as a radioactive tracer in agriculture and medicine. Radiocarbon has contributed immeasurably to our knowledge of living systems and has become an important tool in probing the past, adding greatly to research into both the history of the earth and the history of man.

Credit for the use of radiocarbon in age dating goes to Nobel laureate Willard F. Libby. While at the University of Chicago's Institute for Nuclear Studies, Libby deduced that carbon 14 must be continuously produced in the upper atmosphere by the action of cosmic rays on nitrogen 14, which was known from experiments to be the parent of carbon 14. Combining with atmospheric oxygen to form carbon dioxide, radiocarbon is diffused throughout the environment and eventually becomes incorporated into surface waters and into the tissues of plants and animals. Radiocarbon from the air is also incorporated in limestone and the calcareous shells of invertebrates. When an organism dies, or the precipitation of the lime ceases, the intake of radiocarbon is discontinued and what is already present proceeds to break down steadily to nitrogen 14 with a half-life of about 5,730 years. By measuring the amount of radiocarbon still present, the age of a shell or dead organic material can be determined.

Libby and his collaborators checked the accuracy of their carbon 14 clock with objects of known historic ages—wooden mummy cases, house timbers, and the growth rings of forest trees—and found agreement. The practical upper limit of dating with radiocarbon until recently was about 40,000 years. It is now being extended to more than twice this age.

Originally, it was assumed that the rate of production of carbon 14 in the upper atmosphere remained constant, but it is now known that this assumption was incorrect. In 1958, A. E. de Vries of the Netherlands noted that radiocarbon dates of precisely dated samples from the last 2,000 years were slightly less than dates obtained by counting tree rings. An investigation of this discrepancy was initiated at laboratories of the Universities of Arizona, California, and Pennsylvania. New evidence was provided by precise tree-ring dating of the oldest known living trees, bristlecone pines, in the White Mountains of California. Although these living trees are less than 5,000 years old, the matching of annual growth rings in dead wood was extended in overlapping samples back more than 8,000 years. Bristlecone pine wood decays slowly since it is very resistant to oxidation, insects, and fungi.

Careful radiocarbon dating of ten-year segments of bristlecone wood confirmed that the concentration of carbon 14 in the atmosphere has changed over time. Scientists have developed a detailed correction curve that correlates the chronology of the pines with radiocarbon dates. Archaeological sites have thus been shown to be 200 to 1,000 years older than previous radiocarbon dates had indicated.

A new method of radiometric dating has been devised by geophysicist Richard A. Muller at the University of California at

Berkeley. This method, based on atom counting in a high energy accelerator, can make use of very small samples of any isotopes, including many that could not previously be used. One advantage is said to be an extension of the effective range of radiocarbon back to 100,000 years and more. The older dates, of course, are being cross-checked with other independent evidence such as potassium/argon ratios.

The Paleomagnetic Scale

A major contribution from physics to geochronology is based on variations in the earth's magnetic field. These are recorded in rocks as remanent lines of force established at the time the rocks were deposited as sediments or lava flows.

The earth is a dynamo with a magnetic field produced apparently by movement in the molten part of the metallic core. Laboratory and field observations show how the earth's magnetic field is impressed on the rocks. Sand and silt grains coated with traces of iron, and the crystals of iron-bearing minerals that float in liquid lava are magnetized with uniform intensity and are aligned toward the present magnetic poles. Each individual grain behaves like a compass needle as it comes to rest.

Thus, remanent magnetism in the successive strata of the earth's crust provides a geological record of past magnetic fields and this record shows dramatic changes in the position of the magnetic poles through time.

Navigators have long been aware of a persistent westward drift of the magnetic poles which revolve in tight circles around the axial poles once every 10,000 years. The strength of the field also varies greatly—it is estimated that 1,200 years ago the field was much stronger than now, whereas 5,500 years ago it was much weaker. From the evidence in the rocks it is clear that the field behaves somewhat as does that of the sun; that is, it reverses polarity (direction of magnetism) from time to time. Polarity reversals, which also occur in dynamos of power plants, are not well understood.

Scientists of the Carnegie Institution's Department of Terrestrial Magnetism, while in search a few years ago of information about migrations of the magnetic poles, examined a dated sequence of laminated (varved) lake clays in New England. They made an interesting discovery that the remanent magnetism on successive layers of the clay indicated a shift on the north magnetic pole from the right to the left of true north between 15,000 and 9000 B.C. Pursuing this clue into older rocks in various parts of the United States, they found that paleomagnetic records were strikingly different from the present magnetic field.

Even stronger evidence came from volcanic regions where variations in strength and direction of the magnetic lines were strong and easily traced through successive lava flows. Patrick M. S. Blackett, physicist at the University of Manchester, England, then suggested that not only could the "frozen compass needles" in rocks of all ages be used to write the history of the magnetic field, but that this evidence could also be used to test Wegener's theory of continental drift. Later developments showed his deduction to be right!

By 1967, geophysicists of the United States Geological Survey had determined radiometric ages in lava flows for sixteen reversals extending back more than 4 million years. Because the time lapses between these events were uneven, ranging from less than fifty thousand to more than a million years, reversals could be identified and correlated over the world by their distinctive characteristics, especially their erratic spacing in time, as worked out by geochronological dates. Since the earth's magnetic field is always worldwide, changes in that field are known to affect all parts of the globe simultaneously and can be regarded as indication of synchroneity of events in a global time scale.

According to Allan Cox of Stanford University, a leading investigator of terrestrial magnetism, it turns out that the time required in past episodes to complete a polarity reversal was geologically brief: between one and ten thousand years. During the time of reversals the field never drops to zero, but decreases in intensity by 60 to 80 percent, as it is actually doing now. Creationist spokesmen have another interpretation of the fading of the field: it heralds the end of life within a few thousand years when the magnetic field would no longer protect the surface of the earth from ultraviolet radiation from the sun.

Neil Opdyke, of the Lamont-Doherty Geological Observatory near New York City, showed that the magnetic reversals are readily recognized and enumerated in cylindrical cores brought up from the floor of the deep oceans, where they are interspersed with fossil zones and can be precisely calibrated with radiometric and oxygen isotope data. Correlations of the sequence of strata beneath the sea are now refined by combining all of the various kinds of geochronological information with paleomagnetic stratigraphy. The system is made highly reliable and precise by cross-checking and agreement among the independent kinds of evidence.

Oxygen Isotope Record of Past Climates

Another method of dating sediment sequences in the deep oceans has revolutionized the study of oscillating glacial and

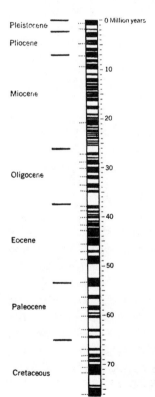

Pleistocene
Pliocene

Miocene

Oligocene

Eocene

Paleocene

Cretaceous

0 Million years

10

20

30

40

50

60

70

Figure 9.2. A record of successive reversals of the earth's magnetic polarity is preserved in sedimentary and lava sequences. Individual reversals are identified by their unequal spacing and duration in time. Normal polarity is shown in black. (National Science Foundation Antarctic Research Program.)

interglacial climatic stages over the past several hundred thousand years. It was conceived by Nobel laureate Harold C. Urey at the University of Chicago.

This is the "oxygen 18" method based on the fact that most of the oxygen atoms in water have an atomic weight of 16, but there are also a few atoms of oxygen 18. As water is concentrated by evaporation the proportion of the heavier isotope increases. For this reason the O^{18}/O^{16} ratio is appreciably higher in normal sea water than in fresh water and it tends to increase with both temperature and salinity. It is interesting to note that the limey shells of aquatic invertebrates possess the same isotope ratios as the surrounding water in which they live.

During the many fluctuations in the volumes of ice caps of the past few hundred thousand years, the alternate build-up and melting of the world's glaciers are recorded by changes in the oxygen ratios of the fossil shells from successive strata under the sea. The sequences of fluctuations in the oxygen isotopes have been found to be worldwide and identical in all ocean basins. Considered with concordant radiocarbon dates and magnetic reversals, they have enabled an international team of scientists (called CLIMAP) to plot precisely the changes in world climates far into the past. The fascinating story of this work is told in a lively way in *Ice Ages* (1979) by John and Katherine Imbrie.

Annual Sedimentary Deposits—Varves

The mud deposited in standing bodies of water in certain cases shows strongly contrasting summer and winter layers. This is true of lakes that freeze over for a few months each year. The annual accumulation, consisting of alternating thin pairs of light and dark-colored sediment, are known as varves. Long sequences of varves equivalent to several tens of thousands of years have been counted and studied in North America and Europe and the contained microfossils analyzed. The results have led to a detailed chronology of climatic changes for late glacial and postglacial times and they have been integrated with concordant radiocarbon dates, much as tree rings have been used as a check on the isotopic ages.

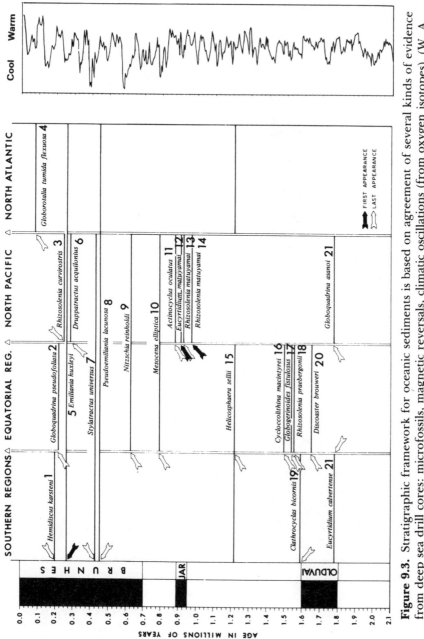

Figure 9.3. Stratigraphic framework for oceanic sediments is based on agreement of several kinds of evidence from deep sea drill cores: microfossils, magnetic reversals, climatic oscillations (from oxygen isotopes). (W. A. Berggren et al. "Towards a Quaternary Time Scale." *Journal of Quaternary Research*, vol. 13, pp. 297–98.)

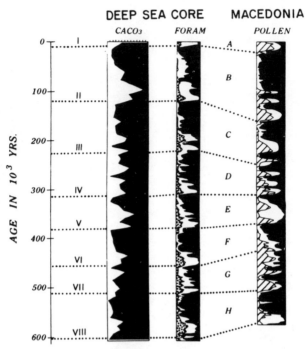

Figure 9.4. Climatic oscillations, recorded in sediment cores, have left their marks simultaneously in both continental and marine sediments. (Courtesy A. McIntyre and J. Imbrie, Lamont-Doherty Geological Observatory.)

Stratification closely resembling varves is also found in modern and ancient marine sediments, caused not by freezing and thawing but by the annual blooming of microscopic organisms in basins of stagnant bottom conditions. Some of these form continuous sequences of hundreds of thousands of varves in rocks of Carboniferous and Permian age.

Banding similar to varves also is formed in glacial ice. In 1972, a team of U.S. Army Cold Regions investigators summarized several years' work on ice cores taken from the thick icecaps of Greenland and Antarctica (*Nature,* February 25, 1972). Both glaciers gave bottom dates well before the last worldwide glacial stage. A more recent Greenland boring in ice reached to a depth of over 2 kilometers with a count of more than 100,000 annual

Figure 9.5. Varves in clay from a New York lake mark the passage of time. Light layers are summer deposits and dark layers are winter deposits. The portion of a core shown is about 30 cm. high. (American Museum of Natural History.)

deposits. Many of the great volcanic eruptions of history were identified from ash frozen in successive layers of the ice.

Corals as Timekeepers

Studies of growth in fossil corals have made a fascinating contribution to geochronology involving past ocean tides and the inferred relationship between the earth and the moon. The moon pulls ocean water in a tidal bulge which moves westward as the earth rotates toward the east. The tidal drag acts as a brake on the spinning earth, gradually slowing it down. Early in the eighteenth century, Edmund Halley, Astronomer Royal of England, noted that there was a discrepancy between the recorded locations of ancient eclipses of the moon and their predicted places of observation. He pointed out that the differences could be resolved by assuming a slowing down of the rate of rotation of the earth.

Figure 9.6. Edge of an Andean icecap in southern Peru showing annual layers of ice. (L. G. Thompson et al. "Climatic Ice Core Records." *Science*, March 1979, vol. 203. © American Association for the Advancement of Science.)

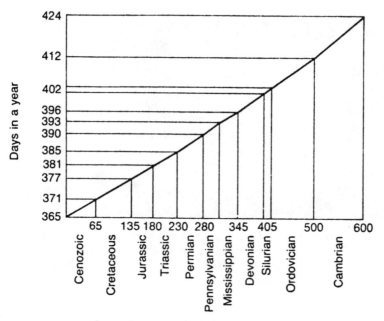

Figure 9.7. Decrease in the number of days per year calculated from slowing of the earth's rotation because of tidal friction. (John W. Wells. "Coral Growth and Geochronometry." *Nature*, 1963, vol. 197, pp. 948–50.)

Modern astronomers have confirmed his theory, and by precise methods have found that the earth is now slowing at the rate of 0.002 seconds per century. This seems very little, but can be appreciable over tens of millions of years.

The slowing of the earth's spin decreases the number of days in the year and causes the moon to draw away from the earth, thus conserving the energy within the earth–moon system. The rate of recession of the moon away from the earth is now calculated at about 5.6 centimeters per year. Until recently there was no way to test these astronomical deductions, but paleontology now provides an independent test.

The discovery was made by John W. Wells at Cornell University, a leading investigator of living and fossil corals. Wells knew that the skeletons of corals (and many other kinds of invertebrates)

Figure 9.8. Daily growth lines of a Devonian coral. By analogy with modern corals these may be grouped statistically into monthly and annual divisions that correspond to oscillations in the tides. (American Museum of Natural History.)

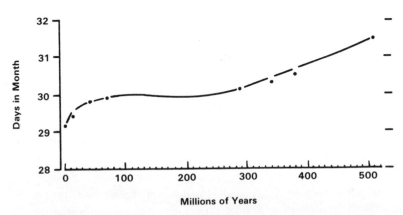

Figure 9.9. Slowing of the earth's rotation as deduced from oscillations in growth rates of fossil corals and molluscs. (G. Pannella et al. "Paleontological Evidence of Variation in Synodic Month." *Science,* November 1969, vol. 162. © American Association for the Advancement of Science.)

display parallel growth rings similar to the annual growth of trees. He was able to show that annual bands of living corals are themselves made of narrow lines which closely correspond to one day's growth.

With his fossil corals, he reported in 1963 that specimens of Devonian age averaged about 400 lines per year, and Carboniferous corals about 380. Subsequent investigations by intrigued paleontologists have shown that the number of daily growth increments per year in corals and molluscs has indeed been decreasing through geological time.

Astronomers had already calculated that average tidal friction would allow 425 days per year in the Cambrian and 400 days per year for the Devonian. As well as providing evidence of close agreement between these two scientific approaches, John Wells'

	Age from Beginning of Unit		% Age of Earth	Duration	
	Cenozoic 65		1.4	65	
	Holocene (Recent)	0.01			0.01
	Pleistocene	2			2
	Pliocene	5			3
	Miocene	22			17
	Oligocene	37			15
	Eocene	53			16
	Paleocene	65			12
Phanerozoic 570	Mesozoic 225		3.5	160	
	Cretaceous	135			70
	Jurassic	190			55
	Triassic	225			35
	Paleozoic 570		7.5	345	
	Permian	280			55
	Carboniferous	345			65
	Devonian	395			50
	Silurian	435			40
	Ordovician	500			65
	Cambrian	570			70
	Precambrian 3800		69.4	3230	
	Ediacaran	700			130
	Lower and Middle	3800			3100
	Hadean 4650		18.2	850	

Figure 9.10. Generalized geochronology in millions of years.

work also provides a measure of the antiquity of fossils in years, totally independent of radiometric methods.

Following up Wells' discovery, Colin T. Scrutton, of the University of Newcastle-upon-Tyne, found what appeared to be monthly bands in Devonian corals equivalent to the intervals between times of the full moon. He calculated 13.03 lunar months in a Devonian year of 399 days. This work has opened up a whole new field of historical research involving the earth—moon relationship.

The creationists, in their narrow interpretation of the Scriptures, have placed their unshakable faith in a very young earth. Consequently, they flatly reject the supporting lines of evidence of geochronology that the earth is enormously old. The bearing that this has on evolution is obvious. A young earth does not provide sufficient time for evolution. The age, as determined by geochronological methods, is ample to explain the evolution of the diversity we see all around us.

10

Diversity and Classification

Organic diversity is a response of living matter to the diversity of environments, and to opportunities for different modes of life on our planet. [Theodosius Dobzhansky, *Genetics and the Evolutionary Process.* New York: Columbia University Press, 1970.]

Some variation is simply an expression of the Creator's desire to show as much beauty of flower, variety of song in birds, or interesting types of behavior in animals as possible. [John N. Moore and Harold Schultz Slusher, eds., *Biology: A Search for Order in Complexity.*]

What is the Meaning of Diversity?

Viewed closely, the rich association of organisms in a tropical rain forest or on a coral reef is awesome in its seemingly endless diversity. The many kinds, sizes, shapes, activities, and microhabitats of living beings are bewildering. Over the world organisms range in size from submicroscopic bacteria to the blue whale, probably the largest animal that ever lived, at 150 tons, with a length of more than 27 meters. After more than two centuries of exploration the number of described living species is now placed at around 1.7 million.

This striking diversity raises many questions. We saw in chapter 8 that life has been highly diverse throughout long spans of time. Creationism holds that the world's plants and animals have been decreasing in diversity by extinction, but the fossil record indicates quite the opposite. As faunas and floras replaced their ancestors through time new organisms appeared more frequently than outmoded groups disappeared. Creationists say that all major groups were created within a span of a few days. The fossil record

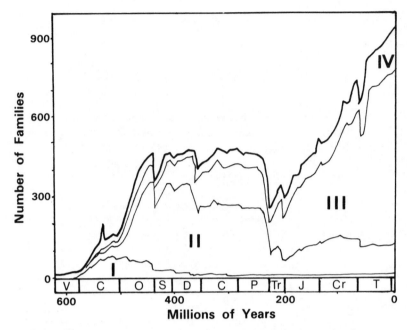

Figure 10.1. Overall diversity of families of fossil marine animals increase through time. I: Families dominant in the Cambrian period. II: Families dominant in the later Paleozoic. III: Families of fossil animals dominant in modern seas. IV: Families of soft-bodied animals rarely preserved as fossils. The build-up to more than 800 families late in geological time is about one half the families known to be living, and the ratio is increasing with new discoveries. Thus, it appears that fossils, at the family level, present a good record of past life. (J. John Sepkoski. "A Factor Analytic Description of the Phanerozoic Record." *Paleobiology*, Winter 1981, p. 49.)

shows that this is far from true. New groups have originated by branching like the limbs of a tree throughout geological time. Table 10.1 is an estimate of the current number of living species known to science, classed in the various major groups.

Best known to the general public are the mammals, about 3,500 species, and the birds, about 9,000 species. These figures are not likely to increase much with new discoveries; in fact, they are decreasing because of accelerated extinctions. Animals are two and a half times as diverse as plants, and the largest single phylum is the arthropods, to which the insects, spiders, and shrimplike

Table 10.1 Estimate of Organism Diversity

Species		Species	
Viruses	300	Animals	
Monera		Invertebrates	
Bacteria	1,700	Sponges	5,000
Blue-Green Algae	1,450	Coelenterates	10,000
Protista		Flatworms	13,000
Protozoans	35,000	Nemerteans	1,000
Slime Molds	400	Rotifers	1,500
Fungi	40,000	Nematodes	50,000
Lower Plants		Annelids	9,300
Brown Algae	40,000	Bryozoans	4,000
Green Algae	2,500	Brachiopods	500
Diatoms and Coccoliths	20,000	Arthropods	1,000,000
Mosses	23,000	Molluscs	120,000
Woody (vascular) plants		Echinoderms	6,000
Ferns	10,000	Protochordates	1,600
Gymnosperms	650	Others	4,000
Angiosperms	280,000	Vertebrates	42,000
Total:	455,000	Total:	1,269,400

animals belong. When the English biologist J.B.S. Haldane learned that around a fifth of all the known species of living organisms are beetles, he remarked: "If I had to say anything about the good Lord, I would say that He must be inordinately fond of beetles."

Less than 3 percent of the species are vertebrates, mainly mammals, birds, and fishes, and 18 percent are land plants, mainly angiosperms (flowering plants). It is fascinating that the latter have a symbiotic partnership with insects, many species of each group being wholly dependent on species of the other group. This interdependence is taken by biologists as an evolutionary phenomenon. Between the two groups they certainly have inherited the earth.

The fossil record shows unequivocally that most, perhaps all, of the early differentiation of life took place in the sea where living conditions were easier than on land. Judged by that record, many major groups have always been confined to the sea, and those that invaded fresh waters and the dry land encountered harsher but more varied opportunities. Paleontologists agree that most species

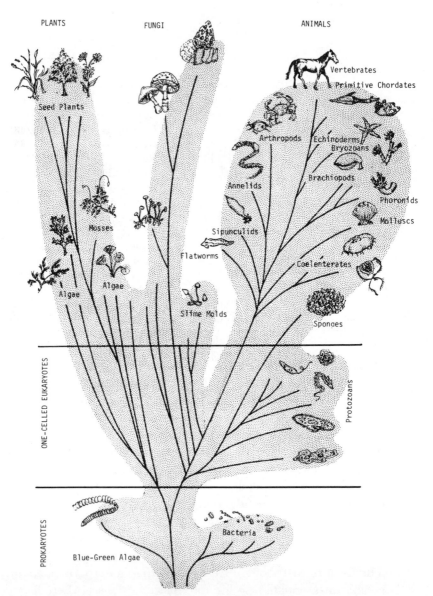

Figure 10.2. Tree of life based on both living and fossil organisms. (Redrawn from Valentine. "The Evolution of Multicellular Plants and Animals." *Scientific American*, September 1978, p. 140.)

Figure 10.3. Major groups of living birds—one example from each of twenty-eight orders. (Adapted and redrawn by permission from J. D. Ebert, A. G. Loewy, R. S. Miller, and H. A. Schneiderman. *Biology*. New York, 1973. © Holt, Rinehart, and Winston.)

of the past are extinct and that the now existing biota is only a fraction of all the kinds of organisms that ever lived.

Thousands of new fossil and living species, mainly small and inconspicuous kinds, are being discovered each year. Some biologists think that the total diversity of life on earth today may run as high as 10 million species. There is a strong probability that many will become extinct because of man's activities before they can even be discovered. The meaning of all this diversity of life is a central concern of evolutionary biology. Small organisms are more diverse than large ones, perhaps because little creatures require a smaller share of the environment than the larger ones.

Professor John J. Lee and his students at City College of the University of New York have done many studies of the microbial communities of Long Island South marshes. They find that a single cubic centimeter of green algae can comfortably accommodate as many as 25,000 micro-organisms belonging to 175 species. Cultured and studied in the laboratory, each species displays its own particular food and other environmental preferences. Even though they live together, they do not use exactly the same resources in the same amounts or ways. The makeup of each community and the behavior of the individual species change with the seasons in response to changes in sunlight, temperatures, and food supplies.

It is interesting that the life zone, or biosphere, reaches from the greatest depths of the ocean, some 11 kilometers beneath the sea level, to 11 kilometers into the air (floating plant spores and bacteria). Live bacteria have also been encountered in oil field brines many thousands of meters underground. The biosphere is sufficiently diverse to provide almost endless opportunities for organisms to share the world's limited life-sustaining resources.

Regional Differences

Since the sixteenth century, biologists have been trying to grapple with a steady stream of newly discovered organisms brought back from exploratory expeditions. The Scriptures had not prepared early naturalists for the many strange creatures that were brought to their attention! Why did the Creator see fit to make so many local kinds of grazing animals when a few widely ranging species would have sufficed? Why was there a different suite of species for every major geographic region? And why did He distribute His flocks and herds in precisely the manner to be expected if they had originated in isolation from one another?

In North America the grazing role was filled by bison and pronghorn antelope, in Australia by more than a hundred species similar to kangaroos, unknown elsewhere. In the New World there were more than three hundred species of hummingbirds, a family previously unknown to Europeans, with a great spread in diverse habitats from Alaska to Patagonia and from lowlands to high mountains. The forests of Australia were found to be unique. They were dominated by more than five hundred species of the eucalyptus family with a great range in form and structure. Elsewhere this group was represented only in nearby New Guinea, obviously by immigrants from Australia. On the other hand,

Australia completely lacked most of the families of trees found on the other continents. In 1761, Buffon reported in his great encyclopedia of natural history that no single species of mammals occurred in both Africa and America and that different areas had different species even in similar environments. Other biologists soon confirmed that this was generally true for both plants and animals of isolated regions, a fact of biogeography that came to be known as Buffon's law.

It is now confirmed that each of the continents, island archipelagos, and even large areas of the oceans have their own distinctive assemblages of species and even many of the higher categories such as families. Hawaii and New Zealand had no mammals excepting bats and rats before the arrival of humans. Likewise, the large island of Madagascar had its own biota unlike those of the nearest continent, Africa. The more remote from each other, the greater the differences between the biology of regions. The small and undistinguished community of plants and animals of Mount Ararat, the supposed place of liberation of animals from the Ark, bore little resemblance to those of most other parts of the world. The Genesis account did not harmonize at all with the facts of distribution of living organisms.

Especially puzzling were the great gaps in geographic distributions of certain organisms. For example, separate species of the rhinoceros were found in Africa south of the Sahara and in far away southeast Asia, and nowhere else. Tapirs of different species lived only in tropical America and southeast Asia; the camel family was restricted to western South America, Asia, and northern Africa. Paleontologists now can show that these and other animals were formerly widely distributed across the intervening areas. Present distributions give little hint of past distributions, which were obviously not wholly controlled by environments, since similar conditions of climate and terrain could be found repeated in the several biological regions. Thoughtful biologists concluded that distribution must reflect past history as well as present environments. This was the point at which paleontology started to make its contributions to a history of life that turned out to be unlike a literal acceptance of the Genesis narrative.

Since observed facts of animal distribution did not agree with

Figure 10.4. Changes in distribution of camels. Fossil remains show that the family probably originated in North America, spread throughout the world, then dwindled to the present (shaded) areas where they live as relicts. (Redrawn and modified from G. G. Simpson and W. S. Beck. *Life.* New York: Harcourt, Brace & World, 1965.)

what would be expected on the basis of special creation or the Flood legend, biologists speculated on the possibility of many centers of dispersal, perhaps even many centers of creation. This kind of thinking was certainly heretical, but the facts were plain and the Bible offered no clarification—perhaps it was better not to think!

Not until the middle of the nineteenth century did Darwin's explanation of the biogeographic regions resolve the problem: the provinces were the result of evolutionary divergence in isolation. Time, varied environments, and geological events had allowed many kinds of plants and animals to become separated and isolated in different areas where they had evolved in separate ways. The facts of this distribution emphatically opposed the idea of a single creation in the Garden of Eden, or the permanence of species.

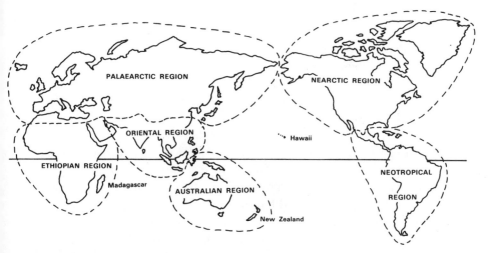

Figure 10.5. The present biogeographic regions based on distinctive animals and plants. Each region is subdivided into provinces and further differentiated by local environments and barriers. (Adapted and redrawn from G. G. Simpson and W. S. Beck. *Life.* New York: Harcourt, Brace & World, 1965.)

Local Differences

Not only are most living species limited in distribution to particular areas but they also are further restricted by the discontinuities of their essential environments within a province. Field studies by many generations of biologists show that every species is delicately attuned to a precise combination of conditions found only in particular places, their habitats and microhabitats. Competition for limited resources requires organisms to adjust (to evolve) in ways that enable them to function efficiently, or they perish. Since environmental conditions are not uniformly distributed, the actual occupancy of a species is a scattered mosaic within its overall geographic range.

It is this specialization for diverse modes of life within regions that greatly enhances species diversity. Organic diversity seems to keep pace with environmental diversity.

Tropical Splendor

Organism communities of temperate climates are simpler and less diverse than those of the tropics. As one moves across climatic belts toward the equator life becomes easier in some respects, productivity becomes continuous and more rapid, and the communities become more varied.

The tropical rain forest is immensely diverse and the interactions of forest organisms with each other and with the physical environment are intricate. Vine-draped trees tower in sheer walls along river banks, and a blanketing canopy of smaller plants clings to trunks and treetops and harbors a wealth of life—insects, birds, reptiles, and small mammals. The vegetation often is so dense that the sky is invisible from the ground. Theodosius Dobzhansky once counted 423 medium-to-large trees in 87 species within a small area of a Brazilian forest of 10,000 square meters. The trees of a temperate forest can be just as crowded, but have a much lower

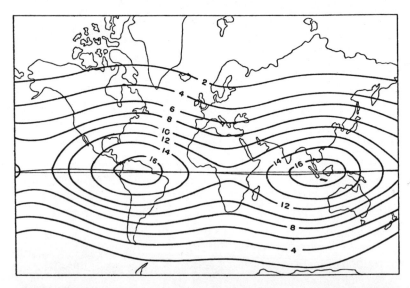

Figure 10.6. Generic diversity of mosquitoes as related to temperature. Similar patterns of increasing diversity toward the equator are displayed by many groups of organisms. (Francis G. Stehli. "Taxonomic Diversity Gradients." In E. T. Drake, ed. *Evolution and Environment.* New Haven: Yale University Press, 1968, p. 172.)

diversity. The striking diversity gradient across climatic belts is taken to be strong evidence of evolutionary accommodation over a long span of time.

Naming Organisms

During the Renaissance, Western scholars rediscovered the works of Aristotle and Plato which gave authority to a primitive and almost universal use of the idea of stylized kinds ("essences," or archetypes) based on familiar animals and plants. This crude method of naming organisms—man, cat, fish, snake—is as old and intuitive as language, but these local names were not adequate for classifying the world's organisms.

The birth and rapid development of systematic biology in the eighteenth century finally called for a scientific system of recording and classifying the growing lists of plants and animals. The Swedish botanist, Carolus Linnaeus, provided the needed system. The outlines of his method appeared in 1735 in two works, *Fundamenta botanica* and *Systema naturae*, which were soon adopted by biologists as the basis for the naming and classifying of fossil and living organisms.

Linnaeus grouped organisms in the order of ascending "importance" from worms to man, whom he named *Homo sapiens* (man, the wise). He then developed a scheme of comparing and grouping animals and plants in an ascending scale of groups based on skeletal and anatomical similarities. He improved on the folk method of giving a single name to the "kinds" of organisms, and instead applied two Latinized names to each organism, a binominal system universally used today.

Linnaeus saw that the diversity of life was extraordinarily orderly, not haphazard, and he believed that he had discovered the grand plan of Creation. Indeed, what he unwittingly discovered were patterns of inherited relationships—something much more fundamental than the groupings of library books or articles in a supermarket. He arranged his units (taxa) in an ascending hierarchical scale with the *species* at the bottom of the list. Like biologists of his day, he did not think in terms of gradations between or within his taxa, and he did not understand organic evolution. He treated species as more or less variable entities, created as we now find them. To him and his colleagues the "kinds" of organisms were the immutable products of divine Creation, as set forth in Genesis.

His method was simple and logical and quickly adopted and amplified by the French biologists Lamarck and Cuvier. Following common experience from human genealogies and stock breeding records, they did not doubt that physical resemblances reflected "bloodlines," and they learned to distinguish between fundamental and superficial resemblances.

The modified Linnaen system in use today may be illustrated by the way in which the domestic dog is placed in progressively more restrictive taxa, from the highest to the lowest categories.

CATEGORY	EXAMPLES
Kingdom Animalia	All animals
Phylum Chordata	With spinal cord, usually with backbone
Class Mammalia	Milk-producing, furry, warm-blooded
Subclass Eutheria	"Placentals," embryo completed in uterus
Order Carnivora	Dogs, cats, bears
Family Canidae	Domestic dogs, wolves, jackals
Genus *Canis*	Domestic dogs, wolves
Species *Canis familiaris*	Domestic dog

Species that are most like each other are grouped together as a genus. Genera are grouped hierarchically into families, families into orders, orders into classes, and classes into phyla. They are natural sets of organisms arranged (by characters in common) in genealogies. We sometimes have trouble defining and recognizing them, but they exist in nature.

Because of the somewhat subjective nature of categories beyond the level of species, it is inevitable that different experts working on a particular group may have different ideas about the best arrangement but, as groups become better known, they become standardized by consensus.

Although creationists shrink from the idea that man is a member of the animal kingdom, they nevertheless accept Linnaean classification as a useful device, but they deny that similarities (even genetical similarities) are necessarily based on heredity. Instead, they speak of the original "kinds" of organisms that were separately created. Any subsequent changes, they say, have been within these original groups. Since the creationists have not settled on an official list of the originally created "kinds" it is impossible to equate their categories with Linnaean taxa except in a context of creationist writings. The dog "kind" seems to be the equivalent of the zoological family Canidae, and a few other families of mammals can be recognized. With invertebrates, however, it appears that each of the many phyla is a single "kind." No new "kinds" have appeared since Creation, they say, and the overall diversity of kinds of life has been dwindling because of extinctions.

Species are Natural Populations

There are two unifying concepts used today in the classification of organisms: heredity and levels of organization. As bearers of heredity, species are fundamental units in studies of evolution and classification, while higher categories are more comprehensive and reflect successive levels of organization.

Early naturalists distinguished species by readily visible (superficial) traits, or "characters." Skeletal and anatomical details came to be considered later, and finally embryological, behavioral, physiological, and biochemical characters were added. All of these are included in the concept of the "phenotype," that is, the biological expression of inheritance. This contrasts with the "genotype" or "genome," the invisible complex of genes that form the line of heredity.

Separate species are reproductively isolated, that is, they usually do not interbreed under natural conditions. This is sometimes incorrectly construed to be a definition of species. Rather, it is an explanation of why they remain separate instead of merging. Since breeding behavior cannot be observed in fossils, emphasis is on general form and structure, that is, "morphology." This is also the most practical method for living species. The visible traits vary in a way that clusters closely around a mean condition. Thus, a species can be described and mathematically characterized from an adequately large sample, and the limits of variation of the whole population can be predicted.

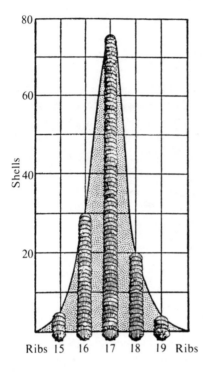

Figure 10.7. Variation in a species of Atlantic scallops. Here, as with most natural phenomena, "random" variation is not chaotic; it falls within definite limits.

Biochemical Characteristics

In the past few decades molecular biologists have found that biochemical methods show great promise for classifying and working out the relationships of organisms. Research in this field has tended to confirm older classifications based on quite different criteria—form, embryology, and geologic history. While the results vary in detail, they strongly support the conclusion that modern classifications are not, as creationists believe, simply arrangements of convenience based on accidental similarities.

Classification and Evolution

The scientific classification of organisms by comparisons of shared characters has brought to biology order out of seeming confusion. Many aspects of the organic world appear disorderly and some attempts by scientists to impose order may be contrived. But when exceptional order is found it leads to inspiring results. The order revealed by modern classifications of organisms eventually led to a theory of relationships and the acceptance of organic evolution of all life from a single ancestor. Classifications of organisms do not merely provide pigeonholes for the filing of information. They reflect heredity and the background of thought that determines the content of evolutionary biology.

11

Heredity and Evolution

What we inherit is a chemically coded message which specifies very exactly the course which the next generation is to pursue. [P. B. Medawar, Nobel laureate, and J. S. Medawar, both English biologists, in *The Life Science*, 1977.]

Underlying similarities of chemical form and structure are consistent with the concept of an all-wise Creator employing a single efficient pattern in his creation . . . and do not necessarily imply an evolutionary origin of life. [John N. Moore and Harold S. Slusher, eds., in *Biology: A Search for Order in Complexity.*]

The Chemical Uniformity of Life

Chemistry provides much evidence that all the major groups of organisms are related by inheritance rather than having arisen independently. Part of this evidence is circumstantial, some is direct, but considered in its entirety it is compelling.

For example, it is interesting to note that only six out of the ninety-two chemical elements make up almost 99 percent of the tissues of organisms: oxygen, 70 percent; carbon, 18 percent; hydrogen, 10.5 percent; nitrogen, 0.3 percent; sulfur, 0.05 percent; phosphorus, 0.04 percent.

The most important of these elements is carbon, unsurpassed in the variety and complexity of its compounds. The connection between the chemistry of carbon and life lies in the remarkable facility with which simple carbon molecules come together to form long, extremely complex molecules known as polymers. These can be produced artificially in the laboratory and by living organisms, but the products from the two sources are subtly different.

More than a century ago, Louis Pasteur discovered that carbon molecules are asymmetrical, some being twisted to the left (L isomers) and others to the right (D isomers). Although the two are chemically identical they can be distinguished by the manner in which they affect transmitted light. The two types of carbon molecules occur together in equal numbers in inorganic compounds of carbon, and as a result they are optically inactive, or "racemic." Most organic carbon compounds, on the other hand, are composed of only one isomer and therefore are optically active. The proteins, for example, which are the most significant constituents of living tissues, are all composed of L isomers. After death, these isomers are slowly racemized, that is, over thousands of years they gradually become optically inactive. This change in racemization can be used in evaluating geologic dating. Since there appears to be no advantage of one symmetry over the other, biologists surmise that the choice of symmetries at the beginning of life may have been arbitrary and that subsequently symmetries have been inherited from ancestors.

Additional important chemical elements which interact with the macromolecules of cells occur in cells and body fluids. Among these are sodium, potassium, calcium, magnesium, and chlorine. These five elements are especially interesting because their relative proportions in organisms as diverse as man, fish, and crustaceans are remarkably constant. Since they are also approximately in the same proportions as those in sea water, biologists infer that this relationship was inherited from ancestors that lived in the sea.

The Basic Unit of Life: The Cell

The basic unit of any organism is the cell. Essentially, it is a chemical factory in which the many fundamental life processes are carried out. Bacteria and protists consist of single cells, whereas the bodies of adult human beings are each said to contain some 60 trillion cells, all stemming from successive divisions extending back to one initial cell, the fertilized egg, to which two parents have equally contributed their heredity.

Living cells conform to a basic plan and have functions common to all organisms. Biologists consider this essential sameness as evidence of kinship, but creationists see it as proof of divine planning. In spite of the fundamental properties all cells have in common, they vary greatly in size and appearance, multicellular organisms having groups of specialized cells that form distinctive tissues such as muscles and nerves.

In all organisms cells perform the same basic functions in much the same ways. They assimilate raw materials from the environment and with these they manufacture a great variety of complex chemical compounds. Instructed by their genes, the cells divide at just the right times and in the right manner to grow into a flower, a tree, or a pretty girl.

There are two different kinds of cells, one more complex than the other. The simple, prokaryote cells (illustrated by bacteria) lack a nucleus and other distinctive parts (organelles). More highly organized organisms are composed of more elaborate eukaryote cells which have one or more nuclei and elaborate internal organelles of several kinds, all with distinct functions. In these a chemical substance, ATP (the same in all animals and plants), is manufactured in one of the organelles for the transfer of energy.

Two organelles, chloroplasts and mitochondria, are especially interesting to those who study evolution, for both contain their own genetic systems which are unlike the cells in which they function. They originate by divisions of earlier chloroplasts and mitochondria, and in many ways resemble independent micro-organisms. Biologists believe they originated long ago as bacteria before they became incorporated in eukaryotic cells in a permanent symbiosis, surely an immensely creative step in the history of life.

A similar deduction applies to the cilia of protists and certain cells of metazoans. Cilia (and flagella) are fine, whiplike cell appendages which all have the same basic construction throughout the organic world. Each cilium consists of an outer ring of nine pairs of microtubules surrounding two axial tubules. This remarkable structure is found in the windpipes of humans and other animals, the pumping cells of sponges, the swimming organelles of microbes and spermatozoans, and the cells of mucous membranes throughout the animal kingdom. Before the invention of the electron microscope, cilia were thought to be integral parts of

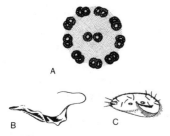

Figure 11.1. The complex structure of cilia and flagella is closely similar in all kinds of organisms. *A*: Diagrammatic cross-section, greatly enlarged. The two central tubules are surrounded by a cylinder of nine doublets consisting of a complete tubule and an embracing, incomplete, tubule. *B*, *C*: Micro-organisms illustrating a whiplike flagellum and multiple cilia.

the cells that bear them. Modern studies show, however, that they resemble spirochete bacteria and could well represent a symbiosis of those bacteria with eukaryotic cells acquired in the early history of life before the origin of multicellular organisms.

Genetic Machinery

Our understanding of the nature and mechanisms of heredity is one of the most remarkable intellectual achievements in human history. Thousands of years of practical experience in the domestication of plants and animals made people aware in a general way that "like begets like," and that ancestral traits are inherited. Actually, offspring differ from their parents, and it is just this difference that enabled our ancestors to cultivate new varieties of domestic plants and animals.

The fascinating story of genetics begins with the work of Gregor Mendel, a Moravian monk, in the city of Brno in what is now Czechoslovakia. Mendel cultivated a small monastery garden where he carried out meticulous experiments on the hybridization of peas—experiments that threw the first light on the true nature of heredity.

Before Mendel it was universally believed that heredity was carried by the blood and that the two "bloods" of parents are blended in offspring. As an echo from the past we still speak of "bloodlines" of horses. Mendel showed that traits are inherited through particles (genes) that do not blend, but are segregated in the sex cells and retain their genetic individuality generation after generation, whether or not they are actively expressed in the appearance of the organisms. He also showed that the genes are brought together more or less randomly (i.e., unpredictably) in the offspring. Later it was discovered that there is not a one-to-one relationship between genes and traits, and what appears to be a single biological trait frequently is under joint control of many genes acting in concert. Conversely, genes may influence several seemingly unrelated characters.

This was the humble beginning of a mathematical science that is of great and ever-increasing importance to man. It has provided understanding of genetic abnormalities, it has led to improved qualities in domestic animals and crops, and it helps us to understand many of the most profound problems of life and its history.

Mendel's epochal laws of heredity were long overlooked. With their rediscovery, in 1900, a theory developed that genes reside in the nucleus in tiny sausage-shaped packages called chromosomes. The chromosome theory of inheritance was developed by Thomas Hunt Morgan and his students at Columbia University between 1910 and 1920 and modern genetics was then well on its way. More recent genetic work is discussed later in this chapter.

The Origin of Sex Cells

The egg and sperm cells of organisms are formed by a remarkable process known as meiosis, in which genes are shuffled about to rebuild the chromosomes. Meiosis is one of several major arguments for the interrelatedness of all sexually reproducing life, both plants and animals.

The chromosomes in every body cell are paired. Before fertilization, the first step in the formation of the sex cells is for the chromosomes to duplicate themselves so that each pair becomes four. Next, they break in several places and exchange segments that are not replicas and these segments reunite at the broken

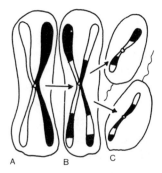

Figure 11.2. Meiosis, the formation of sex cells. *A, B*: The parental pair of chromosomes in a cell exchanges segments. *C*: They then divide to form the sex cells, each of which carries exactly one half of the genetic information in diverse combinations. The mechanism of variability is universal in all sexually reproducing (eukaryotic) organisms.

ends. This first stage in meiosis is called "crossing over" and the result is a complex preliminary shuffling and recombining of the original paternal and maternal genes of each chromosome.

A second division now completes the separation of the original gene pairs and a quartet of sex cells (gametes) is produced, male sperms or egg cells, each of which contains unpaired chromosomes with their unique complement of genes recombined from those present at the beginning of meiosis. In the female, three of the quartet of sex cells are immature and nonfunctional, and only one becomes an egg.

So, the production of genetic variability starts out in recombination when the pairs of chromosomes are reconstituted in a random way. Where n is the number of pairs of chromosomes, the possible combinations vary as 2^n. If there are few chromosomes in the species, the random orientation and segregations lead to less recombination of maternal and paternal genes, but where there are many, as in humans (23), its effect is vast—2^{23}, or 8,388,608 possible combinations of chromosomes in the sex cells. Fertilization of the egg by the sperm squares the number of combinations to over 70 million. The variation is then sharply elevated by the fact that 50 million, or so, sperm per cubic centimeter ordinarily are liberated during human conception although only one lucky sperm with its own individual gene combination is actually used.

It is believed that there are approximately 100,000 pairs of genes in the 23 pairs of human chromosomes. The two members of most of these pairs of genes will be alike (homozygous) and therefore not contributory to variation. If, however, we make a conservative estimate that at least 10 percent (estimates go as high as 60 percent) of the genes are members of a dominant-recessive (heterozygous) pair, the number ($2^n = 2^{10,000}$) is sufficiently vast to enable us to be sure that no two individuals (except identical twins) will be genetically identical. This explains the mystery voiced by philosopher-physician Sir Thomas Browne in 1648: "It is the common wonder of all men how among so many millions of faces there should be none alike."

Mutations

Changes in chromosomes and genes during meiosis frequently produce obscure or conspicuous effects in a developing organism. Such changes, or mutations as they are called, provide another more fundamental source of population diversity. Mostly the mutant cells are faithfully reproduced in subsequent divisions, although some mutations destroy the ability of the cells to replicate. Thriving organisms are, by definition, well adapted and any genetic change may reduce their adaptation for their usual environment while better fitting them for some hypothetical environment.

There are many kinds of mutations observed in a particular species but the range is limited and the frequency of some mutations is much greater than others. In any case, they are unpredictable and there is no evidence that mutation is directional in the sense of evolutionary trends.

Mutation is one of the safeguards against the extinction of a lineage that is confronted by significant changes in the usual environment. Environments change and the variation in any population of organisms resulting from recombinations and mutations of the genetic materials must range widely enough to fit some individuals for new conditions. Otherwise, the species may die out.

The frequency of certain mutations in some organisms seems to be constant, and therefore may itself be under the influence of other genes. In most cases, however, mutation clearly is triggered by unstable environmental factors such as changes in temperature, high-energy radiation, and exposure to certain chemicals.

The appearance of new mutations is not a rare event. It has been estimated that at least one mutation occurs, on the average, per 100,000 genes in every human egg or sperm. Although a mutation of any particular gene may be rare, the appearance of some mutation in an organism is common. Mutant genes may be carried indefinitely as recessives without recognizable effect until two carriers of the same genes mate to produce a double dose in the offspring—the results of which are so-called genetic diseases.

Until recently, the idea of a sudden evolutionary change arising from one or a few mutations was generally rejected as improbable. Even if the bearer of such a mutation could survive to maturity and produce hybrids with a normal mate, so the thinking went, the bearers of the new mutation would be at a disadvantage in competition with normal individuals and would eventually be eliminated. This, however, is not necessarily so.

In plants and some groups of simple animals the chromosome number may be abruptly multiplied during reproduction, an event known as polyploidy. This kind of mutation most commonly is perpetuated only in asexual clones. Some botanists have concluded that nearly one half of the tens of thousands of species of flowering plants may have originated in this way and it appears established that polyploidy is a mechanism by which plants, protists, and the most primitive animals can evolve by steps.

It has become clear that many closely related species do not differ much in their sets of genes. The genetic differences are mainly in the numbers and shapes of their chromosomes, and these apparently are responsible for the reproductive barrier that separates related lineages.

An especially impressive illustration of the importance of chromosomal influence on body form and function are the conspicuous differences in the two sexes of many species that bear only minor chromosomal differences and nearly identical genes. Only a small number of chromosome inversions separate many genera and

Figure 11.3. The horse and zebra bear nearly identical genes but they differ greatly in the number of chromosomes.

families of related forms. Humans, for example, bear twenty-three pairs of chromosomes, whereas apes have twenty-four pairs. One pair of the human chromosomes is larger, formed apparently by the fusion of two pairs of chromosomes similar to the chromosomes of the ape lineage.

Chromosomal mutations are comparatively common in animals, recorded with frequencies of one in a few thousand or tens of thousands of births.

The Chemical Basis of Heredity

In the 1940s and 1950s a remarkable revolution took place in genetics as a result of discoveries that probed deeply into the innermost nature of life and showed why detailed chemical resemblances among living things must reflect their common ancestry.

It had long been known that biological traits are inherited in a set of genes which specify and guide development through a definite sequence of growth stages from birth to old age within limits set by local environments. It was apparent that the potential for every biological trait, from the action of enzymes to eye color, depends on these genes. But what are these genes? This long remained a mystery because they were too small to be directly observed.

The momentous proof that genes are, indeed, chemical bodies, segments of extremely long, folded molecules of a nucleic acid, DNA, came with the work of many investigators. The substance had already been discovered long before, in 1874 by a young Swiss biochemist, Friedrich Miescher, but its extraordinary significance in all life was not appreciated until much later.

Oswald Avery and his coworkers at Rockefeller Institute in New York, Erwin Chargaff at Columbia Presbyterian Medical Center also in New York, and Maurice Wilkins and Rosalind Franklin at London University were responsible for working out most of the chemical details. Then Francis Crick and James D. Watson at Cambridge University fitted the evidence together and deduced the spiral molecular form of DNA and how it perpetuates itself by splitting. Details were filled in later with the electron microscope and other techniques.

Both DNA and its companion RNA are extremely long complex molecules—paired spiral chains, each a "double helix," sometimes compared to a spiral staircase. Normally they have a right-hand twist (B-DNA), but there is also a left-handed variety (Z-DNA). The cross links, or steps, of the DNA staircase are formed by pairs of four kinds of subunits (nucleotides), A, C, G, and T (adenine, cytosine, guanine, and thymine), which alternate in the side strands with sugar and phosphate molecules.

Any group of three of the nucleotides forms a code "word," or codon, which specifies one of the amino acids which are the building blocks of the myriad proteins that make up the cells of organisms. The possible combinations of the 3,000 million nucleotides in a human cell and the gene sequences that they can create seem almost infinite.

The Universal Genetic Code

It is amazing that in all the living world there is only one genetic code based on the four letters A, C, G, and T of the DNA alphabet, and only twenty amino acids are used out of the thousands of known kinds. There is no known reason why just these four nucleotides and twenty amino acids and no others are used, but the favored guess of biologists is simply that the composition of DNA and the amino acid repertory was established early in the history of life and has been inherited by all organisms ever since.

The creationists, of course, would solve this problem in another way. The genetic code was the divine choice among many possibilities at the time of Creation and no further inquiry is needed.

Taking into account sequential order of the nucleotides, there are sixty-four possible combinations. Extra flexibility is achieved by the fact that two or more codon triplets may specify the same amino acid.

DNA does not form proteins directly but transmits its instructions through RNA molecules, most of which lie outside the cell nucleus in tiny granules called ribosomes. It was a form of RNA that provided the clue to the genetic code. Marshall Nirenberg, at the National Institutes of Health in Bethesda, Maryland, discovered and interpreted the triplet code, a remarkable discovery for which he received a Nobel prize. This breakthrough was immediately followed by systematic studies in laboratories over the world of the many codons of RNA to see which proteins they could produce—until finally the codon words for all twenty of the amino acids were discovered.

Let us for a moment compare the DNA molecule with the magnetic tape of a video recorder in which information is stored in coded form in trillions of particles of iron oxide. The performance of a Beethoven symphony by a full orchestra, faithfully recorded both aurally and visually, is stored in a tape to be reproduced at will. To the uninitiated this no doubt is a miracle.

Even more wonderful are the workings of the infinitely smaller DNA molecules by means of which the ancestral genealogy is faithfully replicated trillions of times in the cell divisions of growing organisms when the orchestrated information is played back in the nuances of structure, form, and behavior all molded by the environment.

The Classes of Genes

At first, genes were identified only by their effects, their influence on external form, coloration, and behavior. It is now known that the genes responsible for the manufacture of organic substances, the structural components of the body, are the protein builders. These are the *structural* genes which can be readily identified and mapped chemically by means of their proteins. A second class of genes comprises the *regulator* genes responsible for sequencing all the myriad changes that take place during growth. The structural genes lie in fragments spread out along the DNA molecules and the segments are separated by much longer sequences of DNA whose functions are not so readily determined.

Some segments of DNA behave like units or modules and have the ability to move about and form substitutions in the chains. Considerable scope characterizes the movements of these blocks and they seem to be able to initiate their own movements.

The structural gene fragments are expressed as follows: An RNA exact copy is transcribed of the entire DNA filament that contains the gene segments. The intervening sequences are then eliminated and the gene fragments are brought together. Finally, this abridged RNA molecule, now an exact replica of the gene, moves from the cell nucleus to the ribosomes of the cell where the genetic message is executed and the appropriate protein synthesized.

Neutral Genes

In mammals, 30 to 70 percent of the structural genes consist of repetitive sequences, some repeated hundreds of times. What does this mean? With improved knowledge of protein structure and function it has become apparent that alternative amino acid substitutions in protein molecules are common. Some of these substitutions do not affect their genetic functions and therefore are "neutral."

So many genes seemingly are neutral that evolutionists are now stressing chance genetic and environmental factors in the origin of species, as opposed to natural selection. They feel that natural selection, on the other hand, remains the most important influence leading to adaptation.

Molecular Genealogies

The degree of genetic resemblance between organisms is now accurately measured in terms of the percentages of identical long sequences that they have in common. The differences, which can

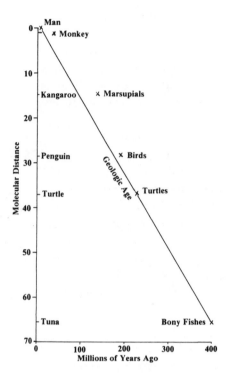

Figure 11.4 The relative distances between certain molecules (cytochrome) on the vertebrate DNA chain (left) are in rough agreement with the spacing of the earliest dates (X) of major vertebrate groups in the fossil record. This agreement is considered corroboration of the times and order in which they originated. (Data from Fitch and Margaliash, *Science*, v. 155, pp. 279–284, 1967.)

be precisely measured, sometimes provide a credible indication of ancestral origins. In figure 11.4 the DNA complex (at left) is analyzed by computer and plotted against the geological age of the oldest known (X) fossil representative of the group. The two sources of information about ancestry are in approximate agreement.

The Chemical Proofs of Evolution

This chapter has been devoted to the common molecular basis of heredity that characterizes the entire organic world. The mechanisms of evolutionary change are found within complex organic molecules which reveal their origins and behave according to the laws of chemistry and biology.

Physical similarities among organisms are closely matched by chemical similarities and from the two lines of evidence evolutionary origins and progress can be plotted. In general, and within the limits of resolution of the fossil record, the biochemical patterns of evolution agree with the stratigraphic sequences of lineages.

The creationist assertion that the observed patterns simply reflect incomprehensible decisions of an "all-wise Creator" is without objective evidence, unscientific, and not essential to a healthy religious outlook.

12

Adaptation: A Question of Design

> Natural selection has often been called another chance
> factor. . . . This is a misapprehension; natural selection
> is an antichance agency. . . . Countless gene combina-
> tions that mutation and sexual combination generate
> are being tried out for adaptedness to the environment.
> [Theodosius Dobzhansky, *Genetics of the Evolutionary
> Process.* New York: Columbia University Press, 1970.]

> *Natural Selection was quietly abandoned, even by its most
> ardent supporters, some years ago.* [Tom Bethell, "Darwin's
> Mistake." *Harper's,* February 6, 1976.]

Divine Purpose?

Plants and animals have the appearance of being tailor-made
for their particular modes of life and there is an obvious correspondence between the way an organism is put together and what
it does. Birds fly, fishes swim, and horses run. The special
adaptations that enable them to engage in these activities have
long suggested to many people that the purposeful aspects of
organisms are evidence that they were specially planned for their
environmental roles.

Leading naturalists from John Ray, in the seventeenth century,
to William Paley, in the nineteenth, wrote books about the loving
care with which God had constructed each and every organism.
Divine planning of the organic world was an obsession with the
theological naturalists, culminating in eight *Bridgewater Treatises,*
published by eminent philosophers and scientists between 1833
and 1840. This ambitious project was intended to illustrate "the
Power, Wisdom, and Goodness of God as manifested in the
Creation." Such was the intellectual environment in which Darwin
began his work. How did the design of organisms come about? By

Figure 12.1. *Hands of an Apostle* by Albrecht Dürer. The five fingers and toes of humans, exquisitely adapted to specialized uses follow a basic plan widespread among the vertebrate animals. But only the apes and monkeys also have nails instead of claws.

chance, by divine decree, or by agencies that might be understood in terms of natural law? What kinds of evidence might be sought?

A religious scientist today is not likely to scoff at the purpose of the *Bridgewater Treatises*, but he might express the thought differently: the manifold examples of exquisite biological constructions that we see on all sides obviously owe their existence to the fact that they are useful to their owners. Complexity and beauty of organisms need not be taken, however, as evidence of design for human enjoyment. Natural processes operating in accordance with natural laws do indeed represent "supreme power," the power of the universe, and the existence of this power is beyond dispute. Whether it is called Nature or God is a matter of personal preference.

Beauty is in the Eyes of the Beholder

Darwin studied plants as well as animals in his search for answers to questions about adaptations. Without questioning divine intent, he showed botanists that the odors, shapes, and colors of blossoms had a single function—to insure fertilization. Different plants accomplished this in different ways. Analysis of their growth and development demonstrated that parts of a blossom corresponded to parts that appeared different in other plants. In other cases the individual parts had different growth origins and different development, but came to have a similar function and appearance in the mature stages. Through endless modifications, flowering plants had developed a partnership with insects, a symbiosis beneficial to both. But the partnership was not indiscriminate. Each insect species in this relationship had its own limited choice of blossoms, and particular flowers attracted only certain insects.

In his book, *Insectivorous Plants*, Charles Darwin reported on the Venus'-flytrap and other animal-trapping plants that had captured the imagination of people as far back as the late eighteenth century. Insects, crustacea, and small frogs make up the diet of these carnivorous plants, among which the most complex type is the "mousetrap" contrivance of the common bladderwort found in marshes throughout the United States. The trap is a small chamber with a door which, when activated by trigger hairs, opens inward, the insect is sucked in, and the door closes and prevents escape. This is one of the most intricate mechanisms in the plant kingdom.

Eventually, thoughts of uniform biological excellence gave way to the realization that organisms, while usually adequately constructed for their particular modes of life, are not consistently well engineered in all their parts. Mostly, they exhibit puzzling imperfections of one sort or another and are subject to genetic ailments that stem from unfavorable combinations and mutations of genes. All suffer from the progressive degeneration which we call aging. Today, biologists recognize in organisms a mosaic of characteristics, some useful, some neutral, and some apparently deleterious, that look as though they had been "improvised," modified from parts that had originally served other purposes. Indeed, this is an unavoidable conclusion, one of many "proofs of evolution," derived from comparative anatomy and embryology where correlated changes in form and function can be directly observed.

An "Urge to Evolve"?

The recognition of organic evolution long preceded the work of Charles Darwin, but no prior scholar had come to grips with the problem of environmental adaptation. Aristotle, Buffon, Robert Chambers, Erasmus Darwin (Charles's grandfather), and many others had speculated about the descent of organisms from a common ancestor, but it was the French biologist, Jean Pierre Baptiste Lamarck, who played the leading pre-Darwinian role in theories of evolution. From 1815 on Lamarck and his followers tried to explain biological similarities and differences as effects of changes brought about by environmental pressures acting directly on individual organisms and passed on to their descendants. The mechanism was vaguely described as an "inner urge" to improve the characteristics of all organisms. In later years this hypothesis came to be known as vitalism, still popular with a few people, mainly nonscientists, who feel that the development of an organism is too complex to be coded in the genes, and that there are so many statistical deviations that there could be no heredity without some unknown force at work. During the early decades of the nineteenth century, when social progress was taken for granted, many evolutionists thought of biological changes, particularly the evolution of man, as directed toward constant improvement to ultimate perfection.

The objection to vitalism and the idea of evolutionary goals is that many generations of optimistic investigators have looked in vain for such evidence. Organisms cannot anticipate their future needs. Claims supporting the so-called inheritance of acquired characteristics are generally rejected as false by countless observations both in the laboratory and in the field. There is a current controversy over the possibility that under narrowly limiting laboratory conditions offspring may inherit immunity to certain diseases from the parent. This possibility has not yet been accepted by a majority of investigators, and in any case it does not affect the conclusion that Lamarckian theory of inheritance has not been a fruitful approach to evolution.

The Awesome Potential of Birth Rates

Darwin had studied medicine at Edinburgh and theology at Cambridge, but he was not specially trained for the life of a field naturalist. Certainly he was not an evolutionist when in 1831, at the age of twenty-two, he was appointed to H.M.S. Beagle for a British naval charting expedition around the world. He spent five years on this memorable expedition, the narrative of which is admirably set forth in his journals and in Alan Moorehead's popular book, *Darwin and the Beagle* (1969). In 1838, an inspiration came to Darwin when he read a work on the growth of human population by the English economist Thomas Robert Malthus. Even before Malthus, Linnaeus had shown by simple arithmetic that any annual plant and its descendants, each producing a minimum of only two seeds per year for twenty years, could, in that brief time, create more than one million progeny (2^{20})!

The same exponential rate of increase applies, of course, to reproduction in human populations which in the 1980s is slowing to a rate that doubles our numbers in only about forty years. But this is small comfort to those who think that the world is already too crowded. At this "modest" rate mankind could produce in two centuries 100,000,000,000 human inhabitants, on a planet that does not now comfortably support 4,000,000,000.

Obviously, thought Darwin, the numbers of any species must be limited by natural means. He was right, for under natural conditions there are, indeed, many environmental checks that prevent organisms from destroying themselves by exhausting their resources. Darwin knew that limiting factors such as food shortages and disease are not applied evenly to most organisms that share resources such as territory, water, food, oxygen, sunlight, and other necessities. Since all organisms considered either as species or individuals are not equally efficient or lucky, some genetic combinations increase more than others. The natural tendency for any population to increase, however, becomes progressively more restrained as its numbers grow and its resources diminish. The brakes are also applied by competition, disease, pollution, predation, and increase in the proportion of old individuals past the age of reproduction. Under such circumstances, populations may reach a steady state when birth and death rates become equal. The point at which this occurs varies with environments and differs with different species.

An Idea is Born

After reading Malthus' book, *An Essay on the Principle of Population*, Darwin believed he had the solution to adaptation. The significant factor was that many of the controls that prevent runaway population could not be haphazard. They clearly were selective. Only the most efficient individuals could, in the long run, live to maturity and pass on their particular traits to future generations. Luck might occasionally favor a poorly adapted parent, but this would be exceptional. Changes in environments could change the picture. Adapted species might have to change biologically with the environment in order to maintain their adaptation, or they would die out. Unchanging species could not survive long, he thought, in a changing world. Darwin termed this sorting process *natural selection*, by analogy with the artificial selection practiced by animal and plant breeders.

After twenty years of gathering evidence, Darwin still would have delayed publication of his conclusions save for a remarkable incident. Early in the summer of 1858, he received a short manuscript from a young biologist in the East Indies, Alfred Russel Wallace, describing an hypothesis of evolution by natural selection identical with his own. Like Darwin, Wallace was acquainted with the rich life of the tropics. He had spent several years in South America and Southeastern Asia and had some experience with geology and fossils. Both men were strongly influenced by the same writers: Malthus, Lyell, and von Humboldt, the German naturalist who had explored the tropical forests of South America.

Evolution had become a common topic of conversation with many people because of a popular but speculative book by Robert Chambers, *Vestiges of the Natural History of Creation*, which posed many unsolved problems. While lying ill with fever, Wallace conceived his hypothesis of natural selection and he wanted to test it with the famous Darwin. Had he not chosen to write Darwin about his idea, we might now be acclaiming Wallace, rather than Darwin, as the founder of evolutionary biology.

Wallace's independent conclusions at first filled Darwin with pangs of disappointment. He had procrastinated too long. Nevertheless, his reaction was extraordinarily generous. On June 18, 1858, he sent Wallace's manuscript to Charles Lyell with the following comment: "If Wallace had my M.S. written out in 1842, he could not have made a better short abstract. Even his terms now stand as heads of my chapters. Please return the M.S., which he does not say he wishes me to publish, but I shall, of course, at once write and offer to send [it] to any journal." Later that year, separate manuscripts by Darwin and Wallace were read before the Linnaean Society, prefaced by joint explanatory remarks by Lyell and Hooker, demonstrating that these friends had known Darwin's view for many years prior to Wallace's independent inspiration. Darwin proceeded to publish his book, *Origin of Species*, in the following year, and Wallace returned to his tropical islands to pursue his work on biogeography. The two men remained close friends as long as they lived, yet not always in full agreement.

Darwin is rightly cited with Copernicus, Newton, and Einstein as a great revolutionary in the history of ideas. He extended the scientific revolution to include living things by his discoveries in the basic causes of evolution. He presented his evidence clearly in a way that captured the imagination of the general public and convinced professional biologists that he was on the right track. People were interested—the legends based on revelation were no longer satisfying to those curious about origins.

Artificial Selection

Many of the arguments for natural selection come directly from the ancient art of domesticating and breeding plants and animals. There are obvious analogies between the two kinds of selection and there are important differences. In domestic breeds, man makes the decisions about what to save and what to eliminate. But, as with nature, he is limited to the gene combinations that naturally appear among prospective parents. He is handicapped by long generation intervals and the low frequency at which viable mutations usually appear—much time is needed. In natural situations it is the environment that determines the result.

Natural selection is less intense than artificial selection, and the changes it produces are much slower. When artificial breeds escape from captivity, they are freed from obligatory inbreeding and, as they are no longer protected, they usually die out in competition with natural populations, or they hybridize with wild relatives and revert to the ancestral type. The special traits desired and cultivated by man generally are not adaptive in natural environments because they are not designed for rigorous natural conditions.

Environmental Tolerance

Since environments are variable, organisms could not survive without being able automatically to adjust to short-term fluctuations in temperature, rainfall, food supply, and other frequent changes. It is a matter of familiar experience that organisms do adjust in many ways to seasonal changes. In regions of temperate climate many animals and plants hibernate in the winter and become inactive during very dry, hot periods. They may even change color, or migrate. All are flexible within rather definite limits while maintaining physiological equilibrium in spite of short-term fluctuations in their surroundings. This phenomenon, called *homeostasis*, as much as any other attribute of organisms gives a purposeful aspect to every living thing.

A defendant of supernaturalism might at this point declare that the entire biological complex shows clear evidence of thoughtful planning and maintenance in the way that Nature provides for, and takes care of, the random elements in the environment. This may give comfort to those already secure in their beliefs, but the evidence indicates that organisms are strictly governed by natural means.

Homeostasis maintains the internal physical and chemical balance of organisms by means of compensatory mechanisms, especially enzyme catalysts, that come into play when environmental shifts occur. In industrial technology such variations are controlled by automatic systems that make adjustments to reduce undesirable effects. These control systems are called cybernetics, and the useful adjustments are "negative feedback." The ordinary thermostat is a good example of such a control system—nothing metaphysical here. The set point of the thermostat determines the level at which changes of temperature will be sensed by the system to start or turn off the operation of the furnace.

The sensors of organisms trigger quick reactions to changes and the reactions may become automatic through conditioning or they may already be incorporated in the genes. They can be slow or fast depending on rates of internal chemical activities. For example, increased heart action accompanies muscular exertion; increased or decreased metabolism maintains uniform body temperature in the face of large fluctuations of external temperatures; and white blood cells and antibodies are mobilized to repel disease germs. The organism may be thought of as a self-setting homeostatically protected machine that can occupy environments within a definite range of variable factors, many of which would be lethal without facilities for maintaining a constant internal environment.

Lamarckians used to think that environmental adjustments were immediately inheritable. They are not. However, as part of the homeostatic responses to changes during growth-development, the vital systems of an organism are kept at an adaptive norm by natural selection. In any species with a high degree of adaptedness and living within a given range of environmental oscillations the genetic endowment of homeostasis is advantageous. Exceptional and extreme variations in a population will be eliminated simply because they are poorly adapted. That is what makes the members of a species similar to one another.

Environmental Niches

The interaction between organism and environment continues throughout life. The building of special structures by animals creates new micro- and megahabitats in which environments can be created or significantly altered—as in the building of bird's nests, beaver dams, and coral reefs. The feeding habits of animals such as elephants, goats, and termites frequently produce profound environmental changes over large areas. Recognition of this inseparable partnership between organisms and their environments directs attention to the ecological nature of adaptation.

The environmental setting of a species (e.g., lake, swamp, sea, forest) is the habitat, while the *niche* is its lifestyle—its activities, the kinds and amounts of resources that it uses, and the methods by which it obtains them. The niche of each organism is unique and another species cannot exactly duplicate it. Where there is appreciable overlap of niches one normal effect of competition for resources is for reduction of overlap through behavioral changes.

The diverse species of mammals, birds, and insects of the Serengeti wildlife preserve, in Tanzania, have been intensively studied from the standpoint of their interrelations. They manage to coexist on what would seem to be resources used by too many. It has been found that the animals have developed comparatively noncompetitive ways of utilizing different kinds, different growth stages, and even different parts of many species of grasses, shrubs, and trees. Seasonal migrations of various species are staggered to accommodate to rainfall patterns and phases of the vegetation. The grazing behavior is such that the same area of vegetation is shared selectively; different species feed on different species of vegetation and on different parts of the same vegetation. The result is a mosaic of healthy, close-cropped, patches of grasses interspersed with other patches of long-stemmed grasses, scattered clumps of shrubs of different kinds, and trees. It has been determined that the growth of vegetation under existing conditions is faster and the production of feed and biomass greater with this community of mixed species than it would be if the vegetation were left untouched or if it were reserved solely for domestic herds and flocks. The niche partitioning evidently is the result of long ages of coadaptation of herbivores and vegetation.

One way for organisms to avoid conflict over limited resources is for some species to shift their feeding habits. If new patterns become genetically fixed, the organisms will slip into new niches, the initial step in evolution.

Some organisms are more flexible than others in their choices of forage, that is, they are opportunistic. For example, the rock pigeon, house sparrow, starling, mouse, and cockroach prosper in many man-made environments.

Some well-defined feeding niches become apparent only on close study. For example, the different species of scavenging mammals, birds, and insects of East Africa arrive at a kill at different times and in a definite order. They are specially equipped to utilize and deal with different parts of a carcass. Each species thus occupies a distinct niche and this partitioning of the resource allows them to coexist with a minimum of waste. This and other aspects of East African ecology are described in a beautifully illustrated book by John Reader and Harvey Croze entitled *The Pyramids of Life* (London: Collins, 1977).

Competition

Organisms that live together have to share many of the same resources in differing degrees and, of course, all of those resources are finite. Consequently, although much selection is devoted to avoiding conflict, niches may to some degree overlap. This is a familiar concern to every gardener, farmer, and livestock rancher who must be alert to protect his interests against "competing" pests. In some cases, field ecologists are able to measure directly the relative levels of use of individual resources by comparing selected pairs of competitors, but the problem becomes increasingly difficult as additional species are included in the analysis.

Darwin and Wallace were among the first to understand the evolutionary implications of competition between different species and between individuals of the same species. They knew that biological competition is not a bloody conflict in the usual sense. Rather, it is a matter of unequal *performance*. The outcome generally is determined by depletion of some limiting resource and a quiet decline in numbers of the less lucky, or less efficient competitors— for example, the opportunistic increase of weeds in an untended lawn as the grass mysteriously dwindles away. If I inspect the pigeon, house sparrow, starling, mouse, and cockroach prosper in many man-made environments.

Manhattan telephone directory, I find some 2,000 entries of the family name Johnson but only one of Warschenko. This is a commonplace fact of life. I have no doubt that chance plays a very large role in the inequities of distribution.

Patterns of diversity in migratory land birds illustrate the effects of competitive exclusion. Wherever the number of species of land birds is high, as in the tropical forests, the number of migrant land birds (short-term visitors) is low. This is because many of the resources are already fully divided up by the permanent residents, and no surplus is available for the less well-adapted transients who are unable to compete on equal terms. In their flight patterns the latter actually avoid regions of high diversity of resident birds.

Objections to Natural Selection

After publication of Darwin's book, the implications about man's origin were recognized and widely discussed, even though Darwin made very little reference to this controversial subject in his *Origin of Species*. Natural selection was soon distorted by antievolutionists to mean godlessness, and condemned by some as a license for exploitation of the weak by the strong and discrimination against "inferior" races (social Darwinism).

More sophisticated critics compared natural selection to a sieve which selectively eliminates without adding anything new. This idea has been both vigorously defended and contradicted by voluminous observations on natural and laboratory populations. More subtle objections are technical arguments based on the realization that the mechanisms of evolution are much more complex than Darwin knew. Yet there are hardly any evolutionists who would now dispense completely with natural selection as an essential ingredient in a larger theory of evolution.

Selection of both individuals and species plays the role of pruning communities of organisms. But it also performs the creative function of favoring certain genetic combinations over others. In both kinds of selection it is the whole organism that is selected, not just particular traits, or genes.

Frequently voiced objections to natural selection are that "it

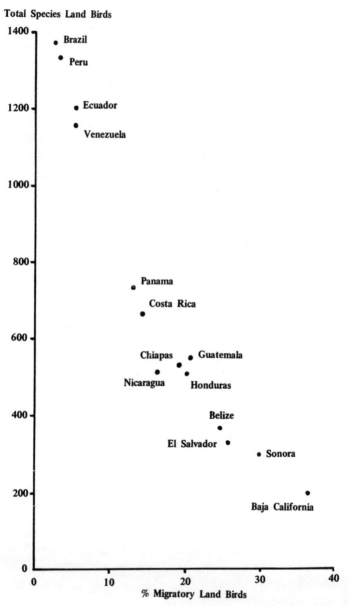

Figure 12.2. The number of kinds of bird migrants decreases toward the tropics in part because niches there are crowded. (Data from Paul Slud, Smithsonian Institution.)

seems to explain anything you want because it is based on circular arguments—organisms survive because they are adapted; they are adapted because they survive." Or, "natural selection is unsatisfactory because it is not capable of being falsified if wrong."

Neither argument is justified. Adaptation and survival are different concepts. The comparative utility of a trait within a particular environmental context can be assessed and the way in which this trait spreads or diminishes in a population is a test of the pressure of natural selection and a measure of adaptation. The documentation of the relationship between natural selection and adaptation must, of course, be made for a specific organism within a carefully defined environment. This can be difficult and laborious, but not impossible.

The creationist stratagem is to insist that natural selection cannot be demonstrated and that leading evolutionists have therefore abandoned it. Consequently, evolution is left without a mechanism. This is a misleading representation of the facts. Virtually all evolutionists assign an important role to natural selection in promoting adaptation, but the limits of its role in evolution are under debate. The real question applies to the part that natural selection plays in the *origin of species.*

13

Structure, Growth, and Form

The variations of the phenotype on which natural selection could act do not arise at random; they are produced by interaction between the organism and the environment during development. [M. W. Ho and P. T. Saunders, "Beyond Neo-Darwinism." *Journal of Theoretical Biology*, 1979.]

Creationists believe that when God created the vertebrates He used a single blueprint for the body plan but varied the plan so that each "kind" would be perfectly equipped to take its place in the wonderful world He created for them. [John N. Moore and Harold S. Slusher, eds., *Biology: A Search for Order in Complexity*.]

Anatomical Similarities

We all know that members of closely knit families of animals such as the cats share many traits. A cat is a cat whether it is a tabby, a puma, or a tiger. Within a single family of organisms the differences usually are mainly proportion, size, and coloration. On the other hand, the differences between two related families, for example cattle and deer, are more pronounced. But even these have much in common that characterize all the members of the larger division to which they both belong, in this case the Order Artiodactyla.

When Darwin was summarizing the biological knowledge of his day he had before him innumerable contributions made by generations of anatomists who had learned to compare the organs and skeletal parts of plants and animals. This method of comparative anatomy was made a major branch of biology by such pre-Darwinian European scholars as Cuvier, Belon, Owen, and even the poet Goethe.

In 1798 Cuvier, when only twenty-nine years old, published his first classification of the animal kingdom based on comparative anatomy. In the course of his life he published many scholarly works on molluscs, fishes, and especially on the skeletons of living and fossil mammals. He showed that each major group has its own body plan, in which the parts can usually be identified with

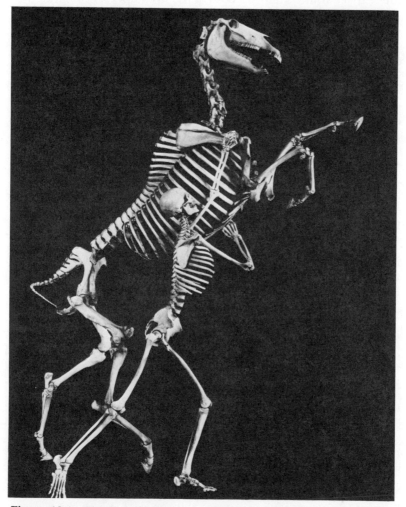

Figure 13.1. The skeleton in all vertebrates has the same basic plan, and bones are almost identical in form in closely related groups. (American Museum of Natural History.)

equivalent parts of even distantly related animals. He showed that the skeletal parts are distinctive for each category of animals because they are intimately related to their functions in the body.

The same (homologous) structures were identified and given the same Latin names even though they varied in size, shape, and even function according to differences in ancestry and modes of life. Cuvier found that the body parts are superbly integrated to work together and, consequently, a species of animal could often be identified accurately from the distinctive shape of even a single part. He showed how to reconstruct whole skeletons from parts based on the observation that bones of a particular shape always occur in the same kind of animal and in the same part of the animal. Paleontologists routinely make use of Cuvier's principles of integration and correspondence of parts to identify and reconstruct the frequently fragmentary skeletons of the past.

The similarities among the members of compact groups like dogs or mice are homologous because they belong to the same closely knit stocks. Examples are the limbs of vertebrate animals which have diverse shapes and frequently do different things, but they develop in the same way during growth and are constructed from the same limited assortment of bones.

Organisms of unrelated groups may also have superficial features in common because they have adapted to similar modes of life which require similar equipment. Take for example the wings of flying animals: birds, pterosaurs, bats, and insects. No common

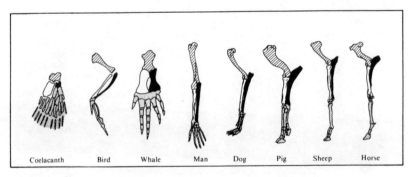

Coelacanth   Bird   Whale   Man   Dog   Pig   Sheep   Horse

Figure 13.2. Matching (homologous) bones of the forelimb in diverse vertebrates. Humerus: ruled; radius: unshaded; ulna: black; wrist and hand (carpals, metacarpals, and digits): stippled.

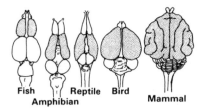

Fish   Reptile Bird
Amphibian   Mammal

Figure 13.3. Homologous regions of the brain in some vertebrates. Cerebrum, the organ of intelligence, is shaded.

ancestor of these animals had wings, so the wings are not homologous and their similarities are termed analogous. Another fascinating example of evolutionary *convergence* on a great scale is that of the Australian marsupials, with many ecological counterparts of the placental mammals of the northern continents.

Functional similarities frequently produce superficially similar structures and forms but the evolutionary changes responsible for this convergence have not modified most of the other complex

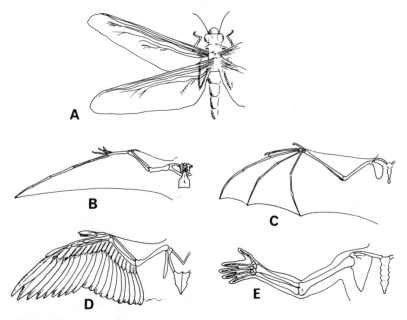

Figure 13.4. Superficially similar structures may have different origins. These forelimbs differ genetically because their possessors do not share the same near ancestors. They are similar because they have become adapted to similar functions. *A:* Insect; *B:* Pterosaur (extinct flying reptile); *C:* Bat (a mammal); *D:* Bird; *E:* Human.

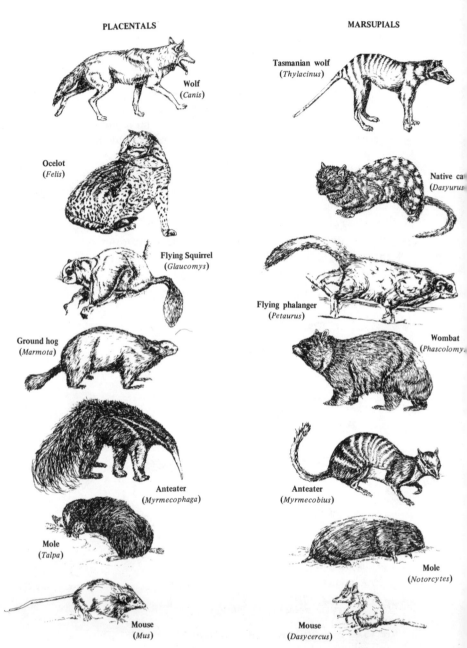

Figure 13.5. Convergence between two groups of distantly related mammals. Although basically unlike in many ways, the two branches have developed a few similar adaptations that fit them for similar modes of life. (Adapted and redrawn from G. G. Simpson and W. S. Beck. *Life.* New York: Harcourt, Brace & World, 1965.)

body parts in the same way. Consequently homologous and analogous similarities are usually readily distinguishable.

Cuvier was not an evolutionist but his methods of comparison eventually persuaded biologists and paleontologists that inheritance from common origins is the only reasonable explanation of the many anatomical similarities among the vertebrates. The same holds for insects, spiders, crustaceans, and all the other invertebrates. Behavior, too, can be homologous—for example, suckling of the young, characteristic of mammals.

The Building of an Organism

Scholars have long pondered the amazing changes that take place in an organism during its life span. From the fertilized egg to adulthood and then senescence, a cycle of development is repeated endlessly by each generation.

The parental genes that guide the sequence of changes particular to each species are handed down to offspring much as a relay racer surrenders a baton to his successor. As may be truly said, "a chicken is the egg's way of making another egg."

In the fourth century B.C., Aristotle made the astute observation, rediscovered long afterward by biologists, that each stage in development is built upon, and is a consequence of, the preceding stage in a cause–effect sequence. Herbert Spencer, a contemporary of Darwin, compared the growth and development of organisms to organic evolution. He felt that it was illogical for people to be opposed to evolution while accepting as a matter of course the even more remarkable processes of growth.

The developmental potential of cells is demonstrated by the way in which the body repairs injuries. Illustrations of this almost universal phenomenon are provided by cuttings of plants that can grow complete bushes or trees capable of producing flowers and fruits; or salamanders and lizards that can regenerate a limb or some other organ that has been lost. The regeneration of parts in experimental animals has become an important field of research in the hope that the healing of, and even the natural replacement of, diseased or injured parts in humans can be accomplished.

Recognition Molecules

The marvels of growth development rest largely on the faculty of all cells to recognize and prefer their own kind. It has been demonstrated that it is their molecular structure that produces this chemical attraction; there is no decision-making or volition involved.

There is an interesting laboratory exercise, sometimes used in elementary zoology courses, that shows how living cells can distinguish foreign substances and recognize their own kind. A living sponge (a very primitive many-celled animal) is squeezed through a mesh so that its cells are separated. Then they behave much like so many individual amoebas searching out the others and reuniting with them to again form the characteristic sponge pattern. Other lowly organisms known as slime molds naturally spend part of their lives as dispersed cells which then come together to form a multicellular organism. Recognition molecules of protein at the cell surfaces have this ability to identify and to join others of their own kind or to reject foreign substances. The same is generally true in sexual fertilization, except that in this case the male cells reject each other and are attracted to female cells of their own species.

Recognition molecules also play an important role in immunity to disease in plants and animals. The defense system is astounding in its versatility and complexity, rejecting whatever is identified as foreign. One example is a body's rejection of transplanted tissues and organs from a donor.

It has been estimated that the human immune system can produce as many as a million kinds of antibodies that can react with as many different antigens. The origin of this antibody diversity has been a puzzle of long standing. It is now thought that it resides in the genes that code for the protein molecules of antibodies.

In the 1960s immunological methods were discovered for comparing the proteins of different animals by measuring their comparative immunological reactions. A protein, say albumin, from animal A is injected into animal B which develops a reaction against the foreign protein. The antibodies produced in the

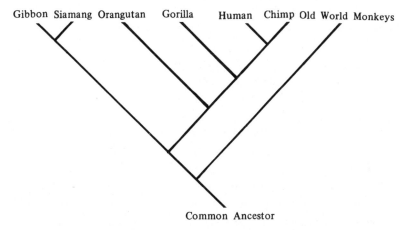

Figure 13.6. Immunological similarities as a biochemical measure of closeness of relationship. Not to scale. (Adapted from Sarich and Wilson. "Immunological Time Scale for Hominid Evolution." *Science*, 1967, vol. 158, p. 1200.)

immunized animal will thereafter react not only against the specific protein (antigen) used but also against proteins of all the relatives of animal A. The greater the similarity between the contrasting proteins the greater will be the immunological reaction. The degrees of dissimilarity between the two proteins are recorded as "immunological distance."

Individual Growth and Development

The search for principles that control the development of an organism throughout its lifetime is a major objective of research in developmental biology, and this search promises to illuminate many of the knotty problems of evolution, especially the origin of form and structure.

One promising lead now under exploration comes from studies of the fruit fly, Drosophila. The mapping of sequences of dividing cells in these insects indicates that the body is divided into growth compartments, or modules, each of which seems to be under the control of a hierarchical system of regulator genes. The modules may be likened to sections along the branches of a tree. At each fork between branches, a regulator gene is turned on in one branch and off in the other. This pattern gives rise to differently situated body parts with different destinations for all the successive cells called for in the DNA blueprint—organs, form, and structure.

The laws regulating the patterns formed by cells during growth are similar in different parts of the body, but it is not yet known how the position-signaling is accomplished. It is evident, however, that the key to differences in form and structure of the body parts does not lie in the cells themselves but in the way they are arranged in the body. The relative positions and varied internal environments of the cells in space and time during successive cell divisions determine how the cells differentiate for different functions. This much is known from experimental work. When tissues are grafted on different parts of the body they frequently take on new characteristics induced by the new situations.

Every organism is a direct outcome of development from an initial cell which takes place in an environmental context which is itself variable. Therefore we can surmise that the developmental system is based in part on hereditary controls and in part on the sequence of events and environmental factors during growth.

The inherent variability of all parts of an organism at all stages in its life was an essential part of Darwin's argument. He adopted the idea that some part of the variation arose from interactions between organisms and their environments and that in some way the results could be transmitted to later generations. He was right, but not in the Lamarckian sense of direct transmission of environmental influences. The genetical basis of heredity was then unknown, but Darwin cited some of the ways in which environmental impact produces variability: muscular development or lack of it, depending on the amount of excercise; the varying effects of nutrition on development; the tanning of fair-skinned people on exposure to the sun; seasonal changes in the foliage of trees, etc. All such variations, he thought, were affected by natural selection wherever they were advantageous or disadvantageous to the individuals that possessed them.

In vertebrates, there are continuous changes in the shapes of bones during growth and development, alterations that are closely related to changing body size and muscular strength. Each bone

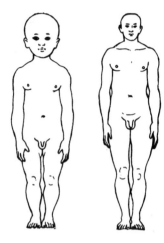

Figure 13.7. Developmental changes. The shapes of child and adult are different. (Gerald Oster. "The Deceiving Eye." *Natural History*, December 1976.)

is remodeled to allow for the differences in proportions and weight of the body. These are nongenetic adjustments to changing intensity and directions of stress. Throughout development, the skeleton is continually modified and integrated in response to mechanical forces.

Cell Sequences

In all but the simplest organisms, the fertilized egg divides scores of times until billions or trillions of cells are precisely arranged in the tissues to create the characteristic forms of all the parts and of the whole adult organism. In the lower vertebrates a hollow ball (the blastula) is first formed from a single layer of cells. One half of this is then tucked in by remarkable cell movements to form a two-layered pouch (the gastrula). Part of the resulting outer layer then changes into a keyhole shaped structure (the neural plate) destined to become the central nervous system. The wide part of the structure develops into the brain and the narrow part forms the spinal cord. In these changes the constituent cells move in a complex pattern and some of them shrink while others divide, finally assuming an overall body shape characteristic of the species to which the animal belongs. Tissue under the neural plate then forms a supporting rod (the notochord) running the length of the embryo under the spinal cord and brain. In placental mammals, such as man, the early embryology is modified by the formation of the placenta, but there are evident parallels with the stages of the lower vertebrates.

Invertebrate embryology follows several different patterns because, unlike the vertebrates, they belong to many phyla. Most invertebrates pass through various ciliated free-swimming larval stages. After completion of this stage, so important in the dispersal of aquatic animals, the larvae settle down to assume shapes of their respective taxonomic groups.

Vestigial Organs

Since many of the organs of animals and plants seem to be modified from previous ancestral conditions in which they were used differently, they might be regarded as vestiges of former conditions. The term *vestigial*, however, is ordinarily limited to organs that apparently have lost their original function (as compared with similar species) and are little used. They are regarded as clues to past evolutionary history.

Many terrestrial invertebrates, for example, show vestiges of aquatic adaptations within the egg. And flightless birds, such as the ostrich and the penguin, have rudimentary wings that clearly are homologous with the wings of other birds. The skeletal

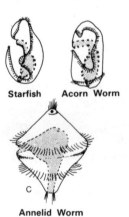

Starfish   **Acorn Worm**

c

Annelid Worm

Figure 13.8. The larvae of diverse phyla of invertebrates display similarities.

structure of the wings of all birds is basically the same and there can be no reasonable doubt that an original ability to fly has been replaced in flightless birds by other means of locomotion.

The python, a large snake, has a greatly reduced, apparently functionless, pelvis and rudimentary hind limbs that are completely concealed within the body, bones which are lacking in other snakes. So far as is known, the adult could function as well, or perhaps even better, without these appendages. Whatever use might be imagined, at least it is certain that pythons do not walk at any stage of life.

Adult baleen whales do not possess teeth, but their embryos do. The embryonic teeth disappear before birth, and during early life a horny "whalebone" filter for sifting small crustaceans grows in the mouth. The baleen whale could not feed on these small organisms without the filter, and teeth would be of no use for this mode of feeding. Thus the baleen filter fits the whale for utilizing a highly abundant and nutritious food source and the embryonic teeth indicate a very different past mode of life.

The fishlike form of seals, manatees, porpoises, and whales does not conceal that they are mammals. In addition to the evidence that they are warm-blooded, suckle their young, and breathe air, they bear many vestiges of organs and skeletal parts used by other mammals for life on land.

Biologists have long suggested that birds had a reptilian ancestor far back in the early Mesozoic. Seemingly confirmatory evidence has been developed by recent work on chicken embryos. Edward J. Kollar and Christopher Fisher, of the University of Connecticut School of Dental Medicine, have succeeded in growing reptilianlike teeth from chick embryos. Their work shows that chickens still possess genes for tooth formation similar to some Jurassic and Cretaceous birds. These investigators think that evolutionary changes in the pattern of embryonic development have turned off the tooth-forming genes rendering all living birds toothless.

Armand Hampé, an experimental embryologist at the University of Strasbourg, recreated reptilian patterns in the leg bones of chick embryos by altering developmental rates. These experiments all show how the function of ancestral genes may change or be discontinued in embryonic development.

Embryonic Resemblances

Early in the nineteenth century, a German anatomist, Karl Ernst von Baer, discovered that the embryos of different adult animals were frequently closely alike and that the specific differences did not appear until the adult stage of development was reached.

Taking into account many lines of evidence, biologists soon concluded that embryonic and later stages of development provided clues to relationships. This idea was amplified and unfortunately distorted by the great German zoologist Ernst Haeckel who concluded that every embryonic stage was like the adult stage of some ancestor. We now know that this cannot be literally true, although there is sometimes an imperfect repetition of ancestral stages (recapitulation) in development.

For those with time and patience to study the facts, embryology falls into place and makes logical evolutionary sense; however, for those creationists who start with the false premise that significantly unlike adult organisms cannot be related, embryonic resemblances must have some other meaning.

No one would think of transforming a fox into a wolf, or a house cat into a tiger. Yet the embryos of these and, indeed, of all mammals are astonishingly alike. Embryonic development shows graphically how different sorts of animals can be derived from very similar embryos. It also shows how minor deviations at any growth stage may become accentuated to produce differences in the adults.

The Timing of Maturity

Changes in body proportions cease in most organisms when they become sexually mature. The exact point in development at

Chick   Calf   Human

Figure 13.9. Diverse vertebrate embryos are similar.

which reproductive activity becomes possible is under the control of regulatory genes that vary in their timing. If sexual development is persistently shifted backward or forward in time the developmental pattern is modified and new traits emerge. If sexual maturity is delayed body changes tend to continue beyond the usual limit and new traits may be added to the adult. Genetic changes that speed up reproductive maturity produce a different result. The adult descendant will then retain some ancestral juvenile traits in the adult stage. This situation, much studied in experimental animals, is known as neoteny. In either case, the organisms will acquire visible, in some cases conspicuous, evolutionary changes that stem from very minor genetic changes.

Old Organs with New Functions

The evolutionary transformation of organs to assume new functions—for example, the change from fins to limbs, or from limbs to wings—involves a minor modification of one developmental pattern into another, a change no more remarkable than the changes that take place in the metamorphosis of a caterpillar into a moth, or a tadpole into a frog.

In the development of individuals as well as the evolution of a

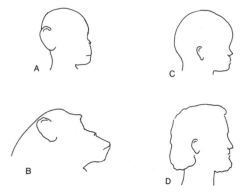

Figure 13.10. The adult skull in modern man has some of the characteristics of the young of other primates. This phenomenon is termed *neoteny*. A, B: Juvenile and adult gorilla. C, D: Juvenile and adult human.

new species, a totally "new" structure does not appear. It is the result of a modification of a pre-existing structure or tissue that assumes a new function unlike that which it served earlier.

Relationships Stem From Common Ancestry

Many converging and concordant lines of evidence point to fundamental relationships among diverse plants and animals. These are much more than the "mere resemblances" of the creationists. Differences among related species, genera, and families are of a higher order than those that distinguish the geographic races of a single species. Outstanding among the clues to relationship among conspicuously different organisms are similar modes of development from the initial cell, homologous structures, similar behavior, and degrees of biochemical resemblance. When relationships are established between higher categories by their joint possession of fundamental characters, it may fairly be concluded that these characters have been inherited from a common ancestor and that the differences are the result of genetical processes of evolution. There can be no other scientific explanation.

14

The Origin of Species

For a biologist the alternative to thinking in evolu-
tionary terms is not to think at all. [P. B. Medawar,
Nobel laureate, and J. S. Medawar in *The Life Science*.
New York: Harper and Row, 1977.]

*Everything was created in six days from nothing. No creation
is observed today.* [Robert E. Kofahl and P. Griffith Lindell,
Creation-Science Research Center pamphlet. San Diego,
California, 1978.]

The Two Levels of Evolution

Those who do research on the mechanics of evolution must
work within a short time scale, perhaps a few hundred generations
in the lives of experimental plants and animals. Most of this work,
called microevolution, has been concerned with the genetics of
changes in both natural races and domestic varieties.

From the great body of observational data on microevolutionary
changes biologists draw analogies for the larger features of evolution of the past—macroevolution. The origin of species is
sometimes considered to lie in the province of microevolution but
changing viewpoints make it necessary to consider speciation (the
origin of species) along with the origins of higher categories, such
as families and orders.

It was long axiomatic with evolutionists that the observed changes
in living organisms, if projected back through tens of millions of
years, could account for the great changes seen in the fossil record
and for the diversity of the living world. Small changes which
continue long enough should result in large changes—a reasonable
assumption. There is now enough evidence, however, to show that
the problems of evolution are more complex than they were

formerly thought to be, and macroevolution may not be simply an extension of microevolution.

Microevolution

Can we see microevolution going on around us? Yes, indeed! Evolutionary processes are apparent in the continuous contests between humans and animal and plant pests, and with diseases, many of which evolve new strains with frustrating frequency. Gonorrhea and malaria, respectively bacterial and protozoal infections once easily held in check by penicillin, aralen, and other drugs, have produced new strains resistant to those remedies. Influenza produces new viral strains as fast as old ones are conquered. Smallpox virus, on the other hand, evidently does not mutate frequently, and consequently that ancient scourge may now have been eradicated, especially since it does not occur in other animals and requires human contact for transmission.

Insects frequently adapt rapidly to changing environments. Formerly, California citrus groves were protected from scale insects by fumigation with hydrocyanic gas. This method was becoming ineffective by 1914, when insect resistance spread rapidly away from central areas as a newly evolved strain extended its territory. Laboratory studies showed that the resistant insects belonged to a genetically new form where emergence was due to differential survival by natural selection of the more resistant individuals, which were transmitting their qualities to new generations of offspring.

In much the same way, new strains of houseflies, lice, and mosquitoes resistant to DDT and other insecticides have been appearing in many parts of the world, and consequently there has been a resurgence of many insect-borne diseases. The U.S. Department of Agriculture reports that of the more than 500 species of insects that do significant damage to crops 267 have built up genetical resistance to insecticides. This physiological evolution by natural selection has taken place within a few decades.

A black mutant of the peppered moth (*Biston betularia*) appeared at Manchester, England, in 1848. Before that date the prevalent form was light gray, but by the end of the century the dark form had almost completely replaced the gray one. The light gray form is almost invisible when resting on light colored lichen-covered tree trunks, but is highly conspicuous on blackened trunks on which the lichens have been destroyed by air pollution. The agent of natural selection here is predation by birds that easily find the light moths on dark trees.

The trend toward a dark color in industrial areas is now reported in more than seventy British species of moths. This trend has been reversed in some areas where there has been extensive industrial conversion to petroleum. The trees have reacquired their normal lighter bark coloration, and selection favors the speckled white variant of the moth. Repeated experiments demonstrate that birds in the two situations prey more on the one or the other variety, depending on how conspicuous they are against a contrasting background.

A well-documented example of rapid microevolution is the spread of the European house sparrow in America. It was introduced in the 1850s and had spread throughout the United States within forty years. By 1948 it occupied virtually all developed parts of North America, always in association with humans. In more than one hundred generations since its introduction, this species has become adapted to diverse local conditions and has differentiated into a large number of distinctive geographic races unlike any of its European ancestors. These local populations are not separate species; they are connected by intermediates and they hybridize. They would certainly, however, become separate species if they became isolated for long periods.

There is some uncertainty about the rate of sparrow differentiation. Some investigators believe that the changes may have occurred early in the first colonization at times of harsh conditions and very high mortality, whereas others believe the changes were gradual. In any case only the hardiest immigrants were tolerant to the new conditions and, as parents, these passed on their special genetic capacities to subsequent generations.

Clive Roots (*Animal Invaders*, 1976) cites a large number of examples of intentional and accidental introductions of organisms by man into new areas. As a result of inbreeding and release from

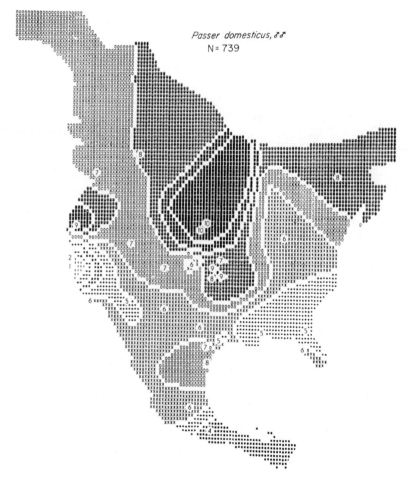

Figure 14.1. Microevolution in the house sparrow. Computer map of the distribution of newly evolved races. (R. F. Johnston and R. K. Selander. "Evolution of the House Sparrow." *Evolution*, March 1971.)

their accustomed environmental constraints, many—like the sparrow—have undergone microevolutionary changes in behavior, physiology, size, form, and coloration.

Without complete isolation, however, microevolutionary changes are likely to be reversible, and such a population cannot split off from other members of its species. Additional processes are needed to produce the great host of species and higher taxa that we see about us.

Reproductive Isolation is the Key to Evolution

It has often been observed that both wild and domestic populations undergo changes when they are permanently subdivided and segregated into small family groups. This is because reproductively separated colonies of organisms cannot exchange genes and therefore accumulate differences. They experience inbreeding among close relatives with the emergence of recessive characters and they usually encounter different local conditions of environment.

If isolation is incomplete, as with the American house sparrow, they still retain contact with other members of their species and they do not diverge enough to form a new species. Instead, they become transient races within larger species populations and freely hybridize when they come together.

The *allopatric* theory of speciation, especially associated with the work of Ernst Mayr of Harvard University, holds that abrupt interruptions in species ranges can initiate changes that lead to new species. For example, populations may send out emigrants that colonize new areas. Or physical barriers are constructed across the original territory of a species: the cutting of canyons, uplift of mountains, drifting apart of continents. These probably are some of the ways that the existing biogeographical provinces became separated.

A well-documented example of a major geological event with a massive effect on evolution was the uplift of the Isthmus of Panama out of the sea in the Pliocene epoch between 3.1 and 3.6 million years ago. At that time, a barrier was formed between the Pacific Ocean and the Caribbean Sea dividing a large number of populations of species into two new biogeographical provinces.

W. A. Newman of Scripps Institution of Oceanography, reporting for a National Research Council committee, reported that of some 15,000 species of marine animals of tropical American seas, not more than 10 percent are now found on the two sides of

Figure 14.2. Emergence from the sea of the Isthmus of Panama divided a continuous marine fauna into two provinces in which the species have since followed different evolutionary paths.

Panama. Most of the species and many of the genera of the two regions evidently have come into existence since that event. This history has been worked out by comparisons of the fossil sequences along Caribbean and Pacific shores and by geochronological methods.

These and other geological events can bring about the protracted physical separation of "founder" populations of individuals. The descendants then continue to change in isolation to fit local conditions. After a few hundred generations the new populations become so different that they will no longer interbreed with the parent population should they reestablish contact. Permanent reproductive incompatibility is established and a new species has been born as a result of segregation and genetic changes.

Fossil Gaps and Macroevolution

In the early days of evolutionary biology, when people viewed the history of life as a gradual ascent of increasingly complex organisms up an evolutionary ladder, it seemed logical to try to arrange living and fossil species in series ranging from simple to complex organisms. This frequently proved to be impossible because the greatest branches, the phyla and most of the classes, appeared to be isolated with only dubious connections. We now know that the connections are there at molecular and embryonic levels. In addition, morphological connecting links between some branching orders, many families and genera, are recognized in both fossil and living forms, and more surely will turn up. These are, indeed, links between diverging chains. It is not necessary to discover every single link, however, in order to recognize the evidence of genealogical continuity.

The many traits of an organism do not all evolve at the same rates and the rates vary from group to group. In much the same way, the similar traits among related members of biological groups do not all show the same degrees of difference. Some traits are nearly identical, others show marked differences. This is the basis of the mosaic patterns of evolution. The nature of the genetic processes renders it virtually impossible for the common ancestor of two major branches to be precisely intermediate in all respects between the derived branches. Transitions accepted by experts are common enough, even though they are generally rejected by creationists.

Abrupt introductions of fossil species in the stratigraphic sequence have been explained in various ways. Alcide d'Orbigny thought that his abundant field observations provided evidence of multiple divine creations that repopulated the world after each of as many catastrophic extinctions. Darwin, on the other hand, thought that the deficiencies were inherent in sedimentary processes. Both interpretations were based on the same scientific evidence. Modern research indicates that most sites of sedimentation, even the deep sea floor, are subjected from time to time to nondeposition or erosion when fossils cannot accumulate. Also, it is common field experience that most rock strata are deficient in identifiable fossils so that it seems that long and continuous fossil sequences without interruptions probably do not exist anywhere.

But these are random situations that do not well explain an almost universal lack of a complete fossil record at the places where we would most like it—at the points of origin of new species.

George Gaylord Simpson, great innovator and one of the founders of modern paleontology, has stressed the unevenness of rates of evolution in fossil lineages. Basing his conclusions in part on the allopatric theory of speciation, he envisioned a "quantum" evolutionary jump to explain the systematic deficiencies of the fossil record. His idea was that evolution is most rapid in small, isolated enclaves, and that these did not contribute much to the fossil record simply because the record is mainly a record of widespread, abundant organisms and therefore is poor in small founder populations. Fossil representatives of small populations certainly are known, however, and many fossil species are known only from single localities, and will probably not be much extended by continued collecting.

There are, of course, other factors to be considered. A connection certainly exists between the size of a population and its genetic stability. The inbreeding of very small, isolated groups can quickly result in a random increase or decrease in some gene frequencies, and especially in the establishment of new mutations shielded from the usual selection pressures of the parent population. These nonselective changes in small populations are accidental. The phenomenon, "genetic drift," was made known especially by the work of the geneticist Sewall Wright at the University of Chicago.

So, the allopatric theory of the origin of species stresses the importance of random situations—population fragmentation, isolation of founder groups, and genetic changes unguided by natural selection. The stages in these changes are all observable in living populations but are rarely identifiable in fossils.

While chance has a large part to play in the origin of species, natural selection will distinguish between those individuals that are adapted and those that are not. This is the nonchance agency of evolution. Subsequent changes due to natural selection complete the speciation process. They occur when the new species escapes from isolation and is confronted by new predators and competitors and a different environment.

If the parent and daughter populations are still not effectively separated by a reproductive barrier the two will hybridize. If they are reproductively isolated they both accommodate to the new relationship and to the new conditions of selection. One of the pair may decline and die out as a result of the competition. Or they may move into different geographic areas or they may adapt to separate environmental niches.

A Modern Theory of Evolution

In the 1930s and 1940s renewed interest in organic evolution brought about a new synthesis embracing especially genetics, paleontology, and systematic biology. Many persons contributed to this but the initial impulse seems to have been that of Theodosius Dobzhansky and Julian Huxley who dubbed the movement the Synthetic Theory of Evolution, sometimes referred to as Neo-Darwinism.

A second revolution in the subject started in the 1970s with the development of molecular biology and studies of the chemical agents of heredity. Paleontologists contributed to this revolution in a significant way. Niles Eldredge and Stephen Jay Gould, of the American Museum of Natural History and Harvard University, respectively, began to stress their growing realization that the Darwinian idea of slow, gradual changes in organisms through time rarely fits the fossil record. Particularly, they pointed to a prevalent and generally overlooked phenomenon—fossil species characteristically persist throughout their range with little change (evolutionary "stasis") after abruptly appearing in the stratigraphic sequence.

The time duration of species indicated in the fossil record varies greatly from less than half a million to many millions of years. In general the more specialized fossil organisms display the shortest

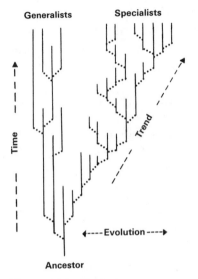

Figure 14.3. Evolutionary patterns according to the theory of punctuated equilibrium. The most significant changes occur during brief periods (thousands of years) of isolation, as indicated by the horizontal bars. These are the speciation events and they are followed by long intervals of little change (equilibrium) as indicated by the vertical bars. Fewer speciation events result in slow evolution and generalized niches. Frequent speciation causes rapid evolution and specialized niches. (Adapted and redrawn from E. S. Vrba. "Evolution, Species and Fossils." *South African Journal of Science*, February 1980, p. 79.)

time spans probably because they are the most vulnerable to environmental changes. The great longevity of some species is striking testimony to the homeostatic controls that enabled them to tolerate changes in their environments.

There is comparatively little evidence of the steady improvement from ancestor to descendant that Darwin envisaged, an erroneous impression that became fixed in the popular mind as to what evolution is all about. Usually new groups appeared sporadically as offshoots from parent groups, most of which continued to survive for a time contemporaneously with the derived groups. Many lineages became extinct.

Less commonly the ancestor was gradually transformed into descendant species or subspecies. Such microevolutionary conti-

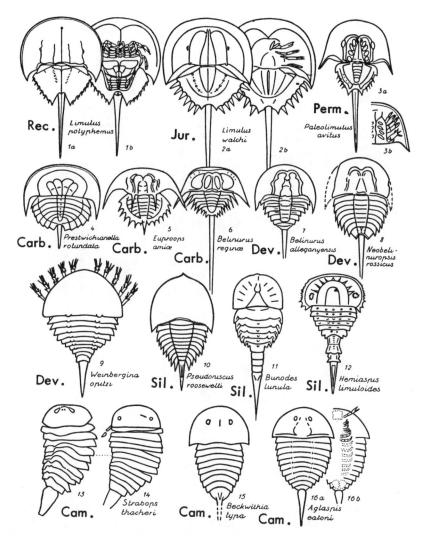

Figure 14.4. Half a billion years of evolution of horseshoe crabs, an extremely conservative group. (After L. Størmer. "Arachnomorpha." *Norske Vidensk.-Akad.*, Oslo, no. 1, 1944.)

nuity within lineages is hard to detect in the fossil record, and even in such examples the incompleteness of sampling usually does not allow an unqualified conclusion that closely spaced speciation events have not occurred.

This de-emphasis on gradualism and natural selection in the

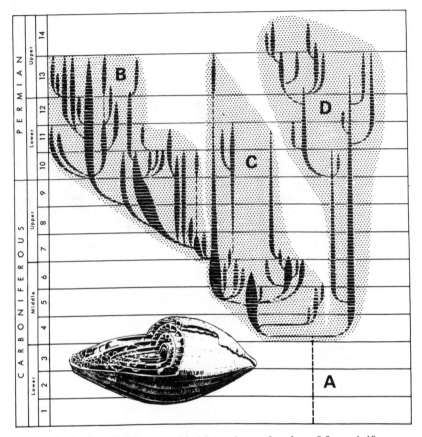

Figure 14.5. Fusulinids, a worldwide extinct suborder of foraminifera of which four families are shown. White bars indicate small gaps in the record. The example shown is about 4 mm. long.

origin of species has gladdened the hearts of creationists, who seem to feel that in some way evolution is being dismantled and left without a mechanism. Quite the contrary! The abrupt and jerky origins of new species, called "punctuated equilibria," refute the basic premise of creationism—that all the species that ever lived came into being more or less simultaneously. Natural selection continues to be the dominant factor in adaptation. It is obvious that a new species must be viable within some accessible environment when it moves out of the confines of its birthplace. Its range of homeostatic tolerance must be adequate to enable it to survive until selection molds its physiology and anatomy into harmony with the new situation.

A species group, i.e., a genus or family, results from several speciation events and the subdivided branches represent increasingly specialized niches. Some of these inevitably will drop out by chance before others. Not all are equally durable or lucky. This is selection at the level of species and determines the characteristics

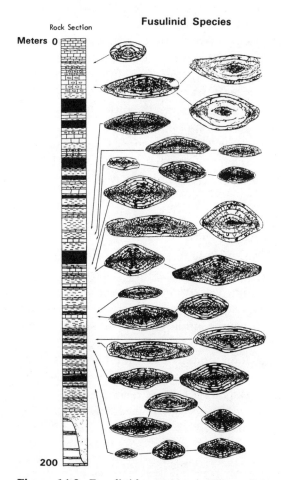

Figure 14.6. Fusulinid sequence in Upper Paleozoic rocks of Kansas. The black bands of the rock sequence represent nonmarine sediments. (M. L. Thompson. *Protozoa*. Art. 5, University of Kansas Paleontological Contributions, 1954).

of higher categories. Chance factors determine the shifts in the environments of species and the environments largely determine the differences in longevity of species. We may assume, however, that survivors have, on the average, some traits in common that give them an advantage and lead to general trends in evolution.

In mass extinctions, such as the decimation of the world biota at the close of the Cretaceous period when the dinosaurs and ammonites and many other major groups disappeared, survivors repopulated the world and formed new communities.

Both Darwin and Wallace failed to distinguish between two quite different kinds of selection—individual selection and species selection—both were included in their original definition of natural selection. Evolutionists now tend to retain the term *natural selection* in a restricted sense for the former, that is, the differential survival of variants within a single breeding population.

Whenever extinction selectively removes species from among a species group, the general character of that group and its history changes accordingly and the changes can be relatively abrupt.

The Origin of Higher Taxa

The origin of any taxon is simply the origin of its split from an ancestral population—a speciation event. The derived species, genus, or family differs from its parent taxon only in possession of some new diagnostic feature which it shares with its own descendants. It need not have undergone extensive genetical reorganization. The new trait may be visually striking or it may be obscure. It takes on taxonomic importance only because it helps define a new group. The taxonomic rank given that group depends on its size, distinctness, and general level of organization.

Evolutionary Trends

Many fossil lineages display trends of increasing complexity and narrower specialization as they are traced upward through the stratigraphic column, but these are exceptional, and others show little change or actually display secondary simplification. Every

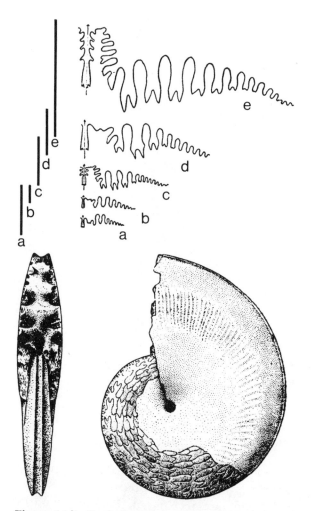

Figure 14.7. Evolution in an Upper Paleozoic family of ammonoid molluscs (Medlicottiidae) during some 65 million years. Overlapping time ranges of five genera are shown by vertical bars. Illustrations are approximately natural size. (Courtesy V. E. Ruzhencev.)

lineage builds on what had proved successful in its ancestors. Unsuccessful lineages simply die out and remove their gene combinations from their group.

A special situation in fossils is the frequent trend for evolutionary increase in size displayed by many groups of organisms (Cope's

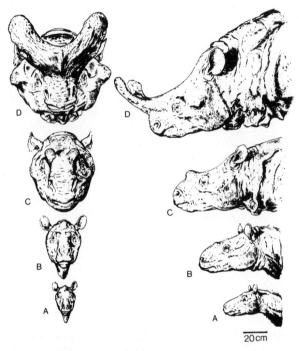

20 cm

Figure 14.8. Titanotheres, an extinct family of mammals that roamed the American Great Plains for about 15 million years in Eocene-Oligocene times. Successive genera are shown in chronological order, the most ancient below. (After Osborn, American Museum of Natural History.)

law). Large size provides certain demonstrated or presumed advantages in competition, protection, and predation.

Where well-defined trends are recognized they attract much attention and are stressed by those who study evolution. But they constitute a minor part of the fossil record, much of which seems to be erratic. Some trends are expressed as parallel sequences in separate but related lineages. Presumably these have undergone similar adaptive solutions to common biological problems. Indeed many of the environmental problems have only a limited number of genetic solutions and this results in a high frequency of similar traits in both related (parallel) and unrelated (convergent) lineages.

Now that my story is told, let me add a brief conclusion to the general subject. The fact that evolution has taken place in the past and is continuing around us still cannot be refuted by any logical arguments. It is the how and why of evolution that are certainly matters for scientific and philosophical discussion.

Some people have a strong emotional aversion to the implications that arise from the concept that humanity is part of nature (not above it), and thus subject to the same natural laws that govern the universe. Recently the news media reported the following outburst from a Georgia judge: "This monkey mythology of Darwin is the cause of permissiveness, promiscuity, pills, prophylactics, perversions, pregnancies, abortions, pornotherapy, pollution, poisoning, and proliferation of crimes of all types" (*Time* magazine, March 16, 1981). Such rhetoric promotes discord and misunderstanding, suggesting that scientific knowledge about human origins is evil.

There are many intangible qualities and values in the world that cannot be thought of in scientific terms—justice, virtue, beauty, and happiness, to name only a few. Among the phenomena that cannot be scientifically measured or explained we must include the events at the initial moment of creation of the universe. Knowledge of the awe-inspiring complexities of organic nature and the universe, with all their grand designs, is daily emerging from the wondering minds of free and dedicated men and women.

Selected References

Alter, Robert. 1981. *The Art of Biblical Narrative*. New York: Basic Books. 195 pp.

Dott, Robert H., Jr., and Roger L. Batten. 1980. *Evolution of the Earth*. 3d ed. New York: McGraw-Hill.

Frye, Roland M. *Is God A Creationist?: Religious Arguments Again Creation Science*. New York: Charles Scribners Sons, 1983, 205 pp.

Gish, Duane T. 1973. *Evolution—The Fossils Say No!* San Diego: Creation-Life Publishers. 129 pp.

Goldsmith, Donald, ed. 1977. *Scientists Confront Velikovsky*. Ithaca, N.Y.: Cornell University Press. 183 pp.

Imbrie, John, and Katherine Palmer Imbrie. 1979. *Ice Ages*. Short Hills, N.J.: Enslow Publishers. 224 pp.

Kusch, David. 1975. *The Bermuda Triangle Mystery Solved*. New York: Warner Books. 317 pp.

Mayr, Ernst. 1978. "Evolution." *Scientific American*, September (Evolution) issue. 242 pp.

Moore, John N., and Harold Schultz Slusher, eds. 1970. *Biology: A Search for Order in Complexity*. Grand Rapids, Mich.: Zondervan Publishing House. 548 pp.

Morris, Henry M., ed. 1974. *Scientific Creationism*. San Diego, Calif.: Creation-Life Publishers. 217 pp.

Nelkin, Dorothy. 1977. *Science Textbook Controversies and the Politics of Equal Time*. Cambridge, Mass: MIT Press. 174 pp.

Slusher, Harold S. 1973. *Critique of Radiometric Dating*. Technical Monograph 2. San Diego, Calif.: Institute for Creation Research. 46 pp.

Stone, Irving. 1941. *Clarence Darrow for the Defense*. Garden City, N.Y.: Doubleday, Doran & Co. 570 pp.

Story, Ronald. 1976. *The Space Gods Revealed*. New York: Harper and Row. 139 pp.

Whitcomb, John C., Jr. 1973. *The World That Perished*. Nutley, N.J.: Presbyterian and Reformed Publishing Co. 155 pp.

White, A. D. 1960. *A History of the Warfare of Science With Theology in Christendom*. 2 vols. New York: Dover. Vol. 1, 415 pp.; vol. 2, 474 pp. (Reprinted from 1896 edition.)

York, D., and R. M. Farquhar. 1972. *The Earth's Age and Geochronology*. Oxford and New York: Pergamon Press. 178 pp.

INDEX

About the Author

Norman D. Newell is Curator Emeritus at the American Museum of Natural History and Professor Emeritus of Columbia University in New York City. His research work in geology and paleontology has taken him to many parts of the world. His studies have been mainly devoted to evolution and the history of life, on which subjects he has published widely. In 1973 when he delivered a lecture to the American Philosophical Society in Philadelphia, he was one of the first of the scientific community publicly to protest the current creationist campaign.

Dr. Newell is a member of the National Academy of Sciences, the American Academy of Arts and Sciences, and the American Philosophical Society. His numerous awards for scientific achievement include those from the National Academy of Sciences, the Philadelphia Academy of Sciences, Yale and Kansas Universities, the Paleontological Society, the Society of Economic Paleontologists and Mineralogists, and the American Museum of Natural History's Gold Medal.

ABOUT THE FOUNDER
OF THIS SERIES

Ruth Nanda Anshen, Ph.D., Fellow of the Royal Society of Arts of London, founded, plans, and edits several distinguished series, including World Perspectives, Religious Perspectives, Credo Perspectives, Perspectives in Humanism, the Science of Culture Series, the Tree of Life Series, and Convergence. She also writes and lectures on the relationship of knowledge to the nature and meaning of man and to his understanding of and place in the universe. Dr. Anshen's book, *The Reality of the Devil: Evil in Man*, a study in the phenomenology of evil demonstrates the interrelationship between good and evil. She has lectured in universities throughout the civilized world on the unity of mind and matter and on the relationship of facts to values. Dr. Anshen is a member of the American Philosophical Association, the History of Science Society, the International Philosophical Society and the Metaphysical Society of America.